LONGING FOR GOD

Orthodox Reflections on Bible, Ethics, and Liturgy

T0324309

Longing for God

ORTHODOX REFLECTIONS ON BIBLE, ETHICS, AND LITURGY

John Breck

ST VLADIMIR'S SEMINARY PRESS
CRESTWOOD, NEW YORK • 2006

Library of Congress Cataloging-in-Publication Data

Breck, John, 1939-
    Longing for God : Orthodox reflections on Bible, ethics, and liturgy /
John Breck.
        p. cm.
    ISBN-13: 978-0-88141-309-0 (alk. paper)
    ISBN-10: 0-88141-309-7 (alk. paper)
        1. Orthodox Eastern Church—Doctrines. 2. Bible—History of
doctrines. 3. Ethics—History of doctrines. 4. Liturgy—History of
doctrines. I. Title.
    BX320.3.B74 2006
    230'.19—dc22

                                                                2006008118

ST VLADIMIR'S SEMINARY PRESS
575 Scarsdale Road, Crestwood, NY 10707
1-800-204-2665
www.svspress.com

ISBN 0-88141-309-7
ISBN 978-088141-309-0

Printed in the United States of America

To the Babes-Bolyai University of Cluj-Napoca, Romania, and especially to its Theological Faculty, in gratitude for the conferring of an Honorary Doctorate.

Contents

IV. OUR LIFE IN CHRIST

Introduction

WITHIN THE DEPTHS OF every human being there exists an insatiable longing for God. This is an inner force, a holy desire or yearning, that can move us out of the torpor of our daily life and lift us to a painful yet sublime level of being, marked equally by sadness and joy. Sadness, because we know very well that in this life the longing will never be fully satisfied, that its object will always remain beyond our grasp. Yet it is a "joyful sadness" (*charmolupē* in the Church's ascetic tradition), because the object we long for reveals itself to be a Person: One who brings us into existence, invites us to seek His face, and draws us into His embrace by continually pouring out upon us His compassion, mercy and love.

The tragedy of our life lies in our constant temptation to lose the focus of that longing and to desire something less than God. Like the ancient Israelites, we repeatedly commit the betrayal of adultery as we go "whoring after other gods." The longing itself becomes perverted, twisted into a self-serving drive for something that will satisfy the corrupted passions rather than nourish the hungry soul.

A strange and powerful restlessness leads us to search beyond our daily life and our immediate experience, in order to find some sense of ultimate meaning and purpose. Wherever we look, however, that restlessness continues to trouble us because our longing goes unsatisfied. Partial fulfillment does come in the form of gratifying personal relationships and accomplishments. We find satisfaction and pleasure in family, friends and enjoyable activities. Yet, even there, the pleasure and the sense of fulfillment are diminished by a terrible yearning. We are consumed by a burning desire for something more, something that touches our heart, something of ineffable beauty that creates in us a response of pure joy. At the same time, we know that this longing for the infinitely beautiful will never in this life be completely fulfilled. Like the Sirens' song, the object of that desire continues to lure us with its heart-breaking loveliness. Nevertheless, it remains a distant and unsatisfied hope, although so intense it brings tears. And the restlessness remains.

As long as that restlessness has no name and no discernable end, we grope and stumble through life looking desperately for something to satisfy us, or at least something to quench the gnawing desire that eats away at us. Unaware that the motor behind that desire is thirst for God, we spend our time and energy chasing after pipedreams and fashioning idols. Yet the dreams remain fantasies and the idols, made of clay, crumble to dust. The ceaseless restlessness leads us again and again to change direction and lose focus. Often we try to escape by opting for what psychologists call a "geographic cure." We pack up and move on to a new town or a new career or a new spouse. Changing our outward circumstances, though, does nothing to change our inner state of frustration and sense of meaninglessness. As the frustration grows, family ties, professional work, recreational activities and other potential sources of satisfaction tend to deteriorate. Because we have lost focus and direction, the restlessness degenerates into anger, anxiety or hopelessness, and we all too easily pass from depression to despair.

Repentance in Christian life is usually thought of as a way to unburden ourselves of guilt. This, though, is only one of its functions. The term "repentance" (*metanoia*) suggests most basically a return, a coming home. It means that we rediscover and relive values and purpose that were given to us at the beginning, when the driving force of authentic longing was first taking shape in our life. Repentance means refocusing that longing in God. It means finding the meaning and purpose of our life in Him, and finding in Him the beauty, the love and the joy we so earnestly desire. Repentance of this kind doesn't just alleviate a sense of guilt and frustration. It transforms that restlessness into an inner quiet, a stillness that fills the mind and heart with a peace which "passes all understanding." Finally, with St Augustine and the entire spiritual tradition of the Church, it leads us to the place where we find our rest, our eternal repose, "in Thee," the One who is the ultimate source and fulfillment of our deepest and most intense longing.

Without that experience of longing, we can have no real sense of *personal* relationship with God. Orthodox Trinitarian theology holds God to be a communion of three Persons—Father, Son and Spirit—united in a single divine essence or nature. The force or impetus that creates and sustains that communion is a sacred longing or desire of One for the Other: a mutual, dispassionate *erōs* that flows from the infinite depths of divine love.

Made in God's image, we reflect something of that love, and the longing that accompanies it. We experience desire for the beloved: a spouse, for example, or a close friend. This feeling or emotion, however, is derivative. The love we feel for another person—when it is deep, genuine and self-giving—is a reflection, however pale, of God's love for us and ours for Him. Authentic love, like authentic longing, is a gift of the Spirit, transcendent in its origin and eternal in its focus. Love and longing originate with God and find their end in Him. Although we are rarely aware of it, the desire and affection we feel for another person are, in their purest forms, expressions of our still deeper longing and love for God.

God, once again, has created in the depths of the human heart a "terrible longing" for Himself. This is a longing to be embraced and filled with the peace and delight of everlasting life in His kingdom, in intimate and unbroken personal communion with the three Persons of the Holy Trinity. It is an all-consuming desire to enjoy forever the peace, the beauty and the glory of God's own Life.

In those rare and precious moments when we can "lay aside all earthly cares," we feel that longing most intensely. Especially in periods when we can enjoy a measure of silence and solitude— to hear the voice of God and to sense most palpably His presence—that longing wells up from our innermost depths, to fill our own mind and heart with the passionless passion of divine *erōs*. This is "erotic love," not in the sense of sexual urgings, but of a burning desire to *know* God and the inexhaustible riches of His mercy and love. It is this insatiable longing that preserves us on the pathway that leads to eternal communion with Him. This longing, too, is the stimulus, the motivating force, that leads us to reject every idol, every proximate goal or selfish ambition, as a vain delusion, and to quest after the true God with faithfulness and perseverance.

This holy longing is the foundational experience of our very being. Without it, we would know nothing but emptiness. Life would be wholly without meaning because it would have no ultimate end, no promise of real and eternal joy. This, sadly, is the condition of most people today, especially in Western societies. We have transferred the focus of our longing to achieving, acquiring and consuming ever more, whether in the form of material goods, enviable reputations or satisfied ambitions. Godly passion has been reduced to lust, just as our thirst for knowledge has degenerated into a need for amusement. Our most passionate quest, in fact, is for entertainment: to be distracted and amused by computer games, Internet pornography, sports events or "must see" TV. Even many of our monks and nuns seek diversions of this kind, attempting to flee from the monotony of a vocation they have never really understood and thus never really accepted. And the rest of us flounder, looking in vain for holy people to model holy lives. Without the impetus of that sacred longing, life is a constant flight from itself. It is perceived and lived out, for those who think about it, as pointless drudgery, a meaningless existence filled with violence, suffering and boredom. Little wonder, then, that our most impassioned social debates today tend to fixate on terrorism, abortion, euthanasia and suicide.

It is possible, nevertheless, to recover a genuine sense of sacred longing. It requires first that we recover a sense of our most basic vocation, which is to exercise our universal priesthood. To renew within ourselves a passionate desire for God that informs and transforms our every thought and gesture, we need to hear once again the assurance of the Psalmist: that the human person is "little less than God," and has dominion over the whole of God's creation (Ps 8). That dominion is exercised primarily by the priestly act of offering. The holy passion of divine longing seizes and inspires us, with all of its joyful sadness, when we accept the call to offer the creation, together with ourselves and one another, to the God who longs to receive and to fill us with His love.

We can make this offering in virtually every moment and every aspect of our life. Each of us, male or female, is created in the divine Image, and with that image is given the potential to serve as a priest. Those ordained to the sacramental priesthood offer up the people and their gifts of bread and wine, in order that those gifts might be transformed and offered back to them as the Body and Blood of Christ. That sacramental gesture, however, is symbolic of the vocation each of us is called to assume as a child of God and bearer of the divine Image. Our vocation is fulfilled most completely and effectively when it issues in offering, when we accept the task of "mediator," by presenting the world to God as we proclaim God to the world.

Insofar as we accept this as our most basic task in life—to make of every relationship and every occupation a priestly offering— then that very acceptance reestablishes an intimate and personal communion with the God we had lost or abandoned. His presence, purpose and love become once again the most significant and precious influences in our life. We discover that indeed "God is with us," at every moment and in every circumstance of life, not to judge or to punish, but to forgive, to bless and to heal.

With this discovery of His loving, saving presence, there invariably comes a rebirth of longing. God once more makes Himself known and experienced in the things, great and small, that make up our daily existence, and we find ourselves drawn inexorably toward Him as the most sublime object of our affection. With this renewed experience we discover as well that life does have meaning and purpose, that the world is not all tragedy, violence and suffering. Then we find ourselves once again compelled and guided, in all that we do and are, by the blessed and terrible passion of holy longing. Repentance consists precisely in this return. Like the Prodigal Son, we head for our true home by placing ourselves and those about us into the open embrace of the Father. And we give thanks for the pain and the joy of that sacred longing, because more than any other experience or influence in our life, it preserves, guides and presses us onwards toward the light, the glory and the joy of our final destination.

This longing, with the priestly vocation it engenders, can shape the way we assume the most important aspects of our daily existence. It can determine how we hear the message of the gospel and how we translate that hearing into social conduct and spiritual worship. Longing is a vital factor in our approach to Scripture, ethics and liturgy, the three chief components of our life in Christ.

Scripture reveals to us the most basic truth about our life: that our longing for God is merely our response to His prior longing for us. It is His prior love (1 Jn 4:10) that creates within us the yearning to know Him and to dwell in Him forever. Read out of this longing for God, the Bible is transformed from a document of antiquity into a wellspring of revelation that provides us with true knowledge of God and thereby with the possibility to share with Him the eternal communion we so ardently desire.

Similarly, that longing restructures the moral life so that it is less deontological than teleological, less grounded in rules and abstract principles than in a quest for personal, intimate and eternal communion with the God of righteousness and love. A genuine hearing of the gospel leads to a deep and sincere desire to conform our life—our thoughts, words and actions—to God's will. Yet it also presses us to express our obedience and devotion by means of worship. It is here, in the liturgical prayer of the gathered Church, that the longing for God becomes most intense and comes closest, in this life, to being fulfilled.

In what follows, our focus will be on Scripture, ethics and liturgical celebration, which together shape our life into a "new creation in Christ" (2 Cor 5:17). We begin with a series of reflections on biblical hermeneutics, and particularly the way the Fathers of the Church interpreted Scripture in their quest for knowledge of God and communion with Him. From there we move on to specific ethical questions that are important for us to consider in a society that has lost its moral bearings under the influence of secularism and a utilitarian approach to medical care. In the third section, we turn to the way Scripture and ethics come to expression in the Church's liturgical life, particularly in the celebration of major feasts that mark crucial moments in the liturgical year. Finally, we explore various aspects of our life in Christ as these are informed by Scripture and Orthodox moral tradition. There we are concerned to review the Church's teaching on the spiritual life, and most specifically on the critical need for silence and solitude. It is by recovering these most basic yet most neglected elements that we can recover as well an appreciation for the indispensable role of *longing* within all of Christian existence.

These brief essays appeared in their original form on the web site of the Orthodox Church in America (*www.oca.org*), under the rubric "Reflections in Christ / Life in Christ." To make up this collection, I have often reworked the articles to provide a more coherent and consistent theme. This book complements an earlier one, also published by St Vladimir's Seminary Press, titled *God With Us: Critical Issues in Christian Life and Faith* (Crestwood, N.Y., 2003). Both volumes are addressed to a popular audience, including students, clergy and laypersons within the Orthodox Christian tradition.

My thanks go especially to the staff of St Vladimir's Seminary Press, for their help and kindness in seeing these works through to publication. I would express my special gratitude as well to Protopresbyter Robert Kondratick, Chancellor of the Orthodox Church in America, and to David Lucs of the Chancery staff, for their unfailing support and encouragement, which made it possible for me to venture into these little explorations.

Particular thanks go to the Babes-Bolyai University in Cluj-Napoca, Romania, and to the members of its Theological Faculty, for their great kindness in granting me a doctorate *honoris causa* in November 2003. This book is dedicated to them, with my most sincere appreciation.

I

The Bible and Its Interpretation

1

Meaning or Meanings of Scripture?

CAN A READER READ THE SAME TEXT TWICE?
This is an odd question, one that has been asked many times since the beginning of this postmodern age. Yet the thought behind it is as ancient as the pre-Socratic philosopher who asked if a person could step twice into the same stream. Now, as then, the answer is both Yes and No.

This is an important question for those who read the Old and New Testament Scriptures, since it provides us with a key to answering other related questions. Just how do those biblical writings convey meaning? And what exactly is the meaning they convey?

Ever since the eighteenth-century Enlightenment, people have tended to become polarized over the issue of reading the Bible. On one side we find "biblical literalists," those who read the sacred writings as though they were primarily history books that present us with a series of facts and events on everything from the creation of the world (in six calendar days) to the Second Coming (with trumpets from Heaven, a place "up there"). On the other side there are scholars who adopt a historical-critical approach that has little confidence in the historical accuracy of biblical texts, but focuses rather on the content and argument of a given writing, the circumstances that gave rise to it, and its function within the community of faith.

Although these approaches seem to be poles apart, they are identical in one major respect. They both assume that the only real meaning to be found in Scripture is the "literal" one. This is usually defined as the meaning "intended" by the biblical author: the sense he understood and attempted to convey. Biblical interpretation (exegesis), therefore, should concentrate on what the text "actually says." From this perspective, the literal sense of the text is typically reduced to its "historical" sense: either "what really happened" (in the eyes of the biblical literalist) or "what the text claims happened" (as discerned by historical criticism).

The earliest Christian theologians, however, knew better than to limit the work of biblical interpretation to either of these extremes. Against a literalist or purely historical approach, for example, Origen in the third century asked rhetorically regarding the creation stories in the book of Genesis: "What intelligent person would believe that the first, second and third day, and the evening and morning, existed without the sun, moon and stars . . . and heaven? And who is so silly as to believe that God, after the manner of a farmer, 'planted a paradise eastward in Eden'?"

This is not skepticism. It affirms rather that biblical accounts often have *more than one meaning*, and that the primary meaning is rarely what is referred to as the "literal" or "historical" sense.

Therefore Origen continues: "When God is said to 'walk in paradise in the cool of the day' and Adam to hide himself behind a tree, I do not think anyone will doubt that these are *figurative expressions* which indicate certain mysteries *through a semblance of history and not through actual event.*"[1]

Nevertheless, Origen, with the whole of the patristic tradition, will see in Scripture historical facts and events as well as figures or symbolic images: facts including the birth of Jesus from a virgin, together with His miracles and His resurrection from the dead. Biblical interpreters of the early Church understood in a "literal" and "historical" way virtually every affirmation that makes

---

[1]*On First Principles* (ed., G. W. Butterworth [New York: Harper & Row, 1966], 288). My emphasis.

up the Nicene Creed. Yet even those affirmations point beyond the literal meaning to a deeper, higher or fuller sense, one that is more spiritual or "mystical." They can be understood not only as statements about what happened in history, but as images of what can transpire in our own life and in the life to come.

Accordingly, the Church Fathers often distinguished between several different senses of Scripture. A good example is the way some of them read the Exodus tradition. In this account of Israel's liberation from slavery in Egypt they found at least four different levels of meaning:

1) the "literal/historical," which speaks of Israel leaving Egypt for the Promised Land;

2) the "allegorical" or "typological," which sees Old Testament images (e.g., Moses and Joshua, the manna and rock in the wilderness) as figures or "types" that are fulfilled in Christ and the Church's sacraments;

3) the "tropological" or moral, which sees in Israel's journey an image of the soul's conversion from sin and death to grace and "newness of life" (Rom 6:4);

4) the "anagogical" or mystical sense, which speaks of the believer's journey toward eternal glory ("anagogical" means "leading upward").

This brings us back to our original question: Can a reader read the same text twice? On the one hand, the answer is Yes. The text (a biblical narrative) is an objective reality in itself. It was produced at a moment in the past and, as canon, it has come down to us in a fixed and immutable form. Although translations may differ, the original (Hebrew or Greek) text remains the same. What we read once we read again, each time we take up the Bible. The words do not change.

The *meaning* of those words, however, can and does change depending on our immediate, personal circumstances and what message, under the guidance of the Spirit, we are seeking in the biblical witness. This will determine which words make an impression on us—and what the text will in fact convey—at any given time. If we read Psalm 22/23, for example, we may encounter Christ the Good Shepherd, who "leads us beside still waters" and restores our soul with His presence, grace and peace. Read it again in times of acute anxiety or before a major operation, and our attention may be drawn to the psalmist's reassuring cry: "Even though I walk through the valley of the shadow of death, Thou art with me!" The psalm has not changed, but our way of reading it most certainly has.

Then again, the way we approach the accounts of Christ's Passion will determine whether we see in the Cross the magnitude of Jesus' physical and emotional agony, or an image of His redemptive sacrifice, or an invitation to struggle and remain faithful to Him through ascetic discipline and works of love, or a promise that "through the Cross, joy has come into all the world," a joy that will be ours as the Risen Lord welcomes us into the glory of His kingdom.

Can we, or do we, read the same text, the same biblical passage, twice or even repeatedly? Yes, insofar as Christ and His Word are the same today, yesterday and forever. Yet no, insofar as the text is a living reality, constantly changing because it is charged with the presence and inspirational power of the Holy Spirit. The Spirit "rewrites" the text, as it were, at every moment of our life, at every step of the tortuous journey that leads us through our daily experience and toward the fullness of life to come.

It is that constant rewriting that makes of the Bible not simply an historical record or a document to be deciphered and analyzed, but a living Word that conveys both truth and life.

2

The Hidden and the Revealed

A N UNACKNOWLEDGED BUT POWERFUL presumption guides a great deal of today's theology, whether it appears in the popular press, in scholarly journals or in Sunday morning homilies. It is the conviction that language and images that depict transcendent rather than empirical reality are mere metaphors. They are "symbols" in the modern, popular sense, which means they are mere "signs" that point beyond themselves to something else. To ancient Christian theologians, on the other hand, words and images are genuinely symbolic: they actually *participate* in the reality they depict. They have the capacity, under the right conditions, to take part in the very existence of the person, object, event or promise to which they refer. It is this capacity that enables words and images to become vehicles of divine revelation.

This understanding of the symbolic character of words and images is basic to Orthodox Christianity. It justifies, and in fact makes necessary, an approach to the interpretation of Scripture that is based to a significant degree on typology. "Types" can be described as verbal images that point forward to future or transcendent realities, as the image of the Hebrew Temple points forward to the Church, the manna in the wilderness to the Bread of Life (of both the Eucharist and the heavenly Banquet), or the Suffering Servant of Isaiah 52–53 to the Person and Passion of Jesus Christ. Because of their symbolic quality, though, types do more than simply point beyond themselves to some future reality, the "antitype." They actually participate in that reality: they share in it and bring it to completion. The Church as the Body of Christ recapitulates and fulfills the covenant relation God had already established with His people Israel; the Eucharist is grounded in and fulfills the Passover liberation of the Exodus, itself symbolized by the blood of the Lamb; and Christ accomplishes His work as Revealer and Redeemer by incarnating—bearing "in the flesh"— the innocent suffering and vicarious death of the Servant of the Lord. Through the relation between Old Testament image and New Testament fulfillment—between type and antitype—God reveals His presence and purpose within the realm of human history, the realm of our daily life.

Typology in the understanding of the Fathers goes farther than this, however. To their mind, the antitype in a very real if mysterious way is already *present* and *active* in the type. This is why the apostle Paul, in 1 Corinthians 10:4, can declare, regarding the rock that followed the people of Israel through the desert to provide them with "living water": "the rock was Christ"!

Because of these connections, exegetes—particularly those interested in "hermeneutics," the principles of biblical interpretation—will speak of Scripture as "self-referential." Its meaning can be grasped, at least in part, by discerning the interrelationships— the symbolic connections—that exist between the Old and New Covenants as between the various books of either Testament. Exegesis, as the Fathers practiced it, involves a constant cross-referencing, from type to antitype, from prophetic image to fulfillment in Christ—and back again (the true meaning of the Hebrew Scriptures, in this perspective, can only be understood as christological: Jesus is both the fulfillment of the Old Testament and the key to its proper interpretation).

To talk in these terms, though, is only possible when we understand two basic truths: that the "ineffable, inconceivable, invisible and incomprehensible"[2] God actually reveals Himself in human

---

[2]These are adjectives taken from the "Anaphora" or Eucharistic prayer of the Liturgy of St John Chrysostom.

history, in the framework of human experience; and that the mode of His self-revelation is essentially that of word and image. (Hence the importance of iconography in Orthodox faith and worship: the words of Scripture are expressed graphically through the dogmatic "statements" of sacred images.)

Theological language, nevertheless, always points beyond itself and beyond the limits of our understanding and experience. Behind every creedal confession, as behind every Gospel account or apostolic exhortation, there lies ultimate, unfathomable mystery, hiddenness. God reveals Himself, He makes Himself known, in the Person of His Son, Jesus Christ. To a limited extent, words and images can capture that self-revelation and present it to us in language that we can understand. Behind the language (verbal or graphic), however, there lies an incomprehensible realm of being, power and glory that the human mind can't begin to fathom, much less express.

God reveals Himself, yet He remains essentially hidden. God calls us to use our intellects to search the Scriptures and to perceive, to understand, His presence and purpose within history and within our life. Yet God remains mystery, inaccessible to thought and inexpressible by means of words or images. Symbols may participate in the reality they signify, but that participation is at best partial. As the ultimate "antitype," Christ may participate—be present and active—in the prophetic images of the Old Testament and in the experience of the Church. But that participation remains "symbolic," real and yet incomplete, until the End-time, the time of fulfillment, when God will be "all in all."

This implies that any interpretation of the Scriptures—whether it serve to deepen our own understanding, to produce formal doctrine, to tell a Bible story, or to preach a sermon—needs to be grounded in an acceptance of the limits of intellectual inquiry, together with an experience of God's self-revelation that is possible only in prayer. St Ephrem the Syrian expresses this point in a verse from one of his Hymns of Faith:

There *is* intellectual enquiry in the Church,
Investigating what is revealed:
The intellect was *not* intended to pry into hidden things.[3]

Each of us is called to investigate what is revealed, and to do so with all the available tools of scientific inquiry. This includes honoring the symbolic nature of language, which enables us to behold in and behind the words and images of Holy Scripture (and of other liturgical, sacramental aspects of our faith) the presence and activity of the God of our salvation. That symbolic language is not mere metaphor. It offers us the possibility to participate directly in the reality it depicts because that Reality is *present* and *acting* in and through the language itself, in and through the words and images that bear witness to it. When we sing the Vespers hymn, "O Gladsome Light," we not only "recall" the image of Christ and the Holy Trinity; we celebrate now—at the "setting of the sun" on *this* day—the presence and glory of God in our midst. When we read and proclaim a biblical story of one of Christ's miracles, we are not merely recalling some event of the distant past. Our "remembrance" occurs in the profoundly biblical sense: it *re-actualizes* what is remembered, so that we ourselves benefit from Christ's ministry: we experience our own healing, accomplished by the unique Physician of our souls and bodies. In similar fashion, when we celebrate the sacraments, our words and gestures enable us to participate immediately in transcendent grace (the ritual of baptism is a true initiation into Christian existence; the wedding crowns, symbolizing both glory and ascetic struggle, actually structure—give shape and direction—to our vocation as a new creation united in "one flesh"). Words, gestures and images have power. They "accomplish what God purposes" in our personal and communal experience (Is 55:10–11).

This understanding of type and symbol is simply lost on most people today, including many who attempt to produce theology.

---

[3]Hymn VIII.9 (trans. Sebastian Brock, *Hymns on Paradise* [Crestwood, N.Y.: St Vladimir's Seminary Press, 1990], 45).

If the traditional theological language of the Church is *theoprepēs*, "worthy of God," it is because it acknowledges and respects the difference between what is revealed and what remains hidden. Yet at the same time, it communicates to us, personally and intimately, the One who reveals Himself out of His infinite hiddenness, to offer us a real and eternal communion in His own transcendent Life and Being.

3
Are the Stories of Jesus' Birth True?

*T*HE CHRISTMAS SEASON INEVITABLY leads people in the media to speculate on whether or not the Gospel accounts of Jesus' conception and birth are historically accurate. The question they raise in the public mind is whether these cherished stories are really "true."

A good, well-balanced example of this kind of reflection appeared in the December 13, 2004, edition of *Newsweek*. The article rehearsed a familiar array of parallels that have been shown to exist between the birth stories concerning Jesus, and those of pagan heroes or demigods. It also showed how the two Gospel narratives of Matthew and Luke (which differ significantly from one another) were structured according to the model of "Promise and Fulfillment." In large part, elements in both accounts were drawn from the Old Testament. Jesus' birth, for example, is patterned after that of Samuel; his descent into Egypt and return to Nazareth recapitulate the Hebrew Exodus tradition; the Magi and their gifts fulfill the prophecies of the Psalms and Isaiah, which declare that kings of the earth shall offer obeisance to the Messiah, sealed by gifts of gold and incense;[4] and the massacre of the children of

---

[4]The myrrh offered by the third Magus, or Wise Man, has a different function. It points forward to the death of Christ and to the myrrh brought to the Tomb by the faithful women. It signals burial but announces resurrection.

Bethlehem reflects the original Passover, when the first-born of the Egyptians succumbed to the angel of death, whereas the Hebrew children were spared by the blood of sacrifice (here Hebrew children are killed, while Jesus, who represents the people of the New Covenant and is Himself the true sacrifice, is spared).

None of the most characteristic events surrounding Jesus' birth—the enrollment under Quirinius, the appearance of the star, the birth from a virgin mother in a Bethlehem stable, the visit of the Magi, the massacre of the innocents, or the descent and return from Egypt—is found elsewhere in historical records. Nor is there any allusion to them in other parts of the New Testament. This leads many scholars to assume that the birth narratives were constructed to create a theological symmetry between the beginning and end of Jesus' earthly existence: He who is finally raised from the dead began His life in an equally miraculously way as the offspring of a virgin mother.

The theological message of these accounts is clear. Jesus is the new and true Israel, the Son of God, who is also "Emmanuel," "God with us." He is no mere prophet, itinerant miracle-worker or firebrand revolutionary, as some have tried to depict him. Rather, He is the fulfillment of all prophecy and the source of all genuine healing. The question that seems to concern us most, however, is this: Are these accounts factually true; that is, did they really happen?

This is a classic example of a false question. To explain why, however, requires that we clear up some common misunderstandings.

In the first place, we tend in our day and age to identify truth with "fact." If an event can hypothetically be recorded on tape or film, if it can be observed and subjected to objective scientific analysis, then we consider it to be true. Such a reality may indeed be factual. Truth, however, is situated on another level, both higher and deeper than the level of fact. Jon Meacham, author of the *Newsweek* article, expressed it very well: "If we dissect the [birth] stories with care, we can see that the Nativity saga is neither fully fanciful nor fully factual but a layered narrative of early tradition and enduring theology, one whose meaning was captured in the words of the fourth-century Nicene Creed: that 'for us men and for our salvation,' Jesus 'came down from heaven, was incarnate of the Holy Ghost and of the Virgin Mary and was made man.'"

"A layered narrative of early tradition and enduring theology." There is no opposition between the two, since (holy) tradition is always shaped to convey theological truth: the significance *for us* of what God has done within the framework of time and space, to work out our salvation. This is why we insist that the Gospels are not books of history but works of theology.

Then again, we need to remember that what we regard as historical facts are never free of interpretation. We know of events such as the beginning of the universe, or the French Revolution or the first Gulf War only as those events have been presented to us by scientists, historians and embedded reporters. We assume their accounts are true, by which we mean factual. The facts that we believe we know, however, are for the most part interpretations we receive in the form of secular "tradition" through media such as news journals, television and books. But like gossip, these interpretations are always colored by the subjective viewpoint, experience and agenda of those who transmit them. We receive and describe even our own personal experiences under the influence of our subjective interpretation of their significance. If I tell other people about some tragic or joyous occurrence I have known, my retelling is always shaped by the impact that experience has had on me. To recount an event or convey a reality is always to interpret it, to pass it through the filter of my own experience and my own understanding. Accordingly, the very notion of "fact," which we so cherish in our age of science and technology, may be little more than an illusion . . .

Yet the Truth will endure forever. However we (or biblical scholars) may judge the historicity of various events, from the Genesis creation account to the narratives of Christ's birth, the truth of those events, and of their interpretations, lies in God's presence and activity in and through them. Genetic engineering has already produced parthenogenesis, or "virgin births," in a Petri dish. But this no more proves the tradition of the Virgin Birth of Jesus than the Shroud of Turin proves His resurrection. The biblical narratives, like the Shroud, are received and interpreted as articles of faith. "Proof," by which we mean objective scientific verification, simply does not apply in their case.

Are the stories of Jesus' birth, as recounted by the evangelists Matthew and Luke, really true? Yes—as affirmed by the faith, but also by the experience, of countless multitudes of people who know Jesus of Nazareth to be Lord and Savior, who pray to Him as God and know their prayer is heard. Yes—because the Church's spiritual elders have always recognized that truth is more than sheer fact, and that Scripture speaks more in the figurative language of poetry than in the analytical language of science. This is because truth is ultimately ineffable. If Scripture resorts to figures and analogies, if the Church Fathers rely so heavily on allegory, and if Jesus expresses some of His most profound teachings in the form of parables, it is because words are symbolic. They point forward to ultimate reality, and they even participate to some degree in that reality. But as human constructs, words are incapable of grasping that reality in all its fullness. This is why the deepest prayer must finally resolve into silence.

Yes, the stories of Jesus' birth are true. They are so, because their purpose and their effect is to convey meaning more than fact. In the final analysis, no particular element of biblical tradition can be definitively proved or disproved. But that doesn't matter. What does matter is the witness that tradition offers us, by means of both historical facts and poetic images, to the significance of the person of Jesus in the whole of God's work to bring to the world salvation and eternal life.

In this light, with the whole of Christian Tradition, we can—indeed we must—declare that in the person of Jesus, the eternal Word of God took flesh and became man. He did so by the power of the Holy Spirit and in the womb of the Virgin Mary. As the "God-man" He suffered, He was crucified and He was buried. Then, on the third day, He rose from the dead in glory, to fulfill the work begun on the first Christmas Eve, in a humble stable in the city of Bethlehem.

With this affirmation historical fact merges with transcendent meaning. To skeptical eyes, none of it can be proven beyond question. To eyes of faith, though, there is no greater reality than this, and no more compelling truth.

4

Scripture: A Verbal Icon

THE LAST CHAPTER TOOK UP THE ISSUE of the relationship between fact and truth in the biblical accounts of Jesus' birth. I tried to point out that the question "Did it really happen that way?" arises from a common misunderstanding that confuses fact with truth, while it overlooks the point that everything reported as fact is filtered through the reporter's own experience and understanding. For that reason, what we receive as fact is always colored and shaped by interpretation: our own, when it is a matter of our personal experience, or that of the person who conveys the information to us.

With regard to the biblical accounts of Jesus' conception and birth, we need to recognize that they represent a synthesis of historical reality—what we call fact—and transcendent meaning, a meaning that human words can express only through images or figures.

We find this synthesis most clearly expressed in Jesus' parables. These are stories built upon common experiences that the hearer knows as fact: the authority of the king or master of the household, the annual cycle of planting and harvesting, the hypocrisy of certain members of Israel's ruling class, the care of a shepherd for his flock, and so forth. Jesus takes these common realities and uses them as images—verbal icons—to express a meaning that speaks to the immediate experience of his hearers. Extrapolating on the basis of their own experiences, those hearers (and future readers of the Gospels) easily see in the king or master an image of God as Lord and Judge, in the agricultural cycle a sign of God's presence and activity in creation, in the rulers of the people a warning of judgment and a call to compassion, and in the shepherd a witness to Christ's own concern to "seek and save the lost."

Jesus never intended for his parables to be taken as fact, in the sense that they recount events that actually took place. They are figures, verbal images, which point beyond themselves to a deeper reality. For that reason, they are more than fact. Although based on familiar daily realities, they lift the hearer to a higher plane, a level of ultimate reality that concerns our relationship with the eternal God.

In this sense, the creation story—indeed, the first eleven chapters—of Genesis can be considered parabolic. If we ask, "Did it really happen that way?", the answer is both Yes and No. Yes, insofar as the creation story of Genesis 1 affirms that God is the unique author of all that exists, that everything comes "from nonexistence into being" by His will and power, and that what He created and continues to create is essentially "good." But no, insofar as it is now known (it is scientifically demonstrable), that the cosmos is not three-tiered with "water above the firmament," and that the "days" of creation cannot be understood literally as 24-hour periods.

To put it in more technical terms, there is a profoundly *mythological* aspect to every biblical account, including the accounts of Christ's Nativity. But to say that, we need to be very clear about the meaning of myth. A myth is not a legend, an invented story. Nor is it to be confused with a parable. In the proper sense of the term, a myth is a narrative that serves to express, in human language and figures, realities that transcend what we consider to be the purely historical. Some realities, such as emotions and aspirations, can be most adequately expressed in the language of poetry.

Transcendent realities—truths about the inner life and external operation of God, for example—can best be expressed in the language of myth.

If this sounds dubious, it is most likely because we tend to misunderstand the concept of history or historical reality. Seduced by a certain intellectual dualism, we create an improper dichotomy between the temporal and the eternal, just as we often do between fact and truth. We consider them to embrace different spheres of reality, whereas they constantly merge into one another. The universe came into being as a result of the "Big Bang." But the reason the question "What existed before that?" cannot be answered is because time itself did not exist. The Creator, however, did exist; and at a particular a-temporal "moment" he set in motion what we know as physical and historical reality. We cannot understand the historical or factual aspect of creation, therefore, without reference to the transcendent Creator (although many people have tried).

Similarly, Jesus' presence in the life and experience of His people occurred in part as a result of certain historically determinable facts, namely that He was born, crucified and buried at specific times and places. Yet at the same time, that birth and that death are transfused with a higher significance because they are vehicles for divine intervention into historical reality. The One born of the Virgin Mary is a human being, but He is also the eternal Son of God; and it is He whose death, followed by His resurrection, marks the definitive Passover into eternal life. Here we find the ultimate merging of time and eternity, of historical event and transcendent truth.

Because God is present and active in every event of world history as He is in our most intimate and personal experiences, it is imperative that we correct any false dichotomy between time and eternity, fact and truth. As we pointed out earlier, however, the respective terms are not synonymous. Truth is always "more" than sheer fact. Yet the two constantly overlap one another: temporal facts are ceaselessly intersected or interpenetrated by eternal truth. All time is permeated with eternity, just as every fact has the capacity to convey some aspect of ultimate reality. Still, eternity transcends time as much as truth transcends simple fact. Language attempts to express this interrelationship, and it does so most effectively in the form of myth: a story in human words that expresses in its own unique way the ultimately inexpressible mystery of divine and human interaction.

This is why we affirm that the Genesis creation story is true, even though every element of the account is not factual. And this explains why the Gospel accounts of Jesus' birth, death, resurrection and glorification are true, although every detail could not have been verified to the satisfaction of skeptics who might have been present. The truth of those accounts, however, is not merely subjective, even though it is perceptible only to eyes of faith. Thomas saw and believed, as did the other disciples, together with countless others (1 Cor 15:3–8!). What they saw was reality: historical reality insofar as they beheld the risen Lord in the flesh, but transcendent reality insofar as that flesh was transfigured into His resurrection body.

Although we are usually oblivious to it, what we call fact, time and historical reality are always filled with eternal presence and meaning. The expression "realized eschatology" is not mere theological jargon. It too is a verbal icon that seeks to express an ineffable truth. It means that the world itself, in the memorable words of Gerard Manley Hopkins, "is charged with the grandeur of God." Scriptural accounts—whether we class them as factual, historical, parabolic or mythological—are verbal icons, whose purpose is to seize that grandeur, to make it intelligible in the form of human language, and to offer it to us as a life-giving witness to what is ultimately and absolutely true.

5

The Ecumenical Conundrum: Divergent Worldviews

T HE ECUMENICAL MOVEMENT SEEMS BLOCKED in an impasse. From its beginnings early in the last century, Protestant and Orthodox Christians have made up the membership of the World Council of Churches, and to the present day bilateral and multilateral dialogues have continued between various Protestant denominations and the canonical Orthodox churches. In recent years, Roman Catholics have joined in the dialogue process, both with Protestants and with the Orthodox. Yet nearly all of the participants are asking just where the movement is headed, as they forge ahead with their conversations, looking for signs of agreement amid diminishing prospects for meaningful unity.

In all, a great deal of good has come from these discussions. Theologians have come to better understand and appreciate Christians of other confessions, and occasionally the papers produced by participants in the dialogues have marked a significant advance toward rediscovering the Apostolic Faith. A recent example is the Roman Catholic / Orthodox agreement on certain aspects of the *filioque* controversy.[5] Yet a gulf still exists between "East" and

---

[5] This refers to the addition to the Nicene-Constantinopolitan Creed of the term *filioque* ("and the Son"), made in the sixth century by Roman Catholic theologians. It concerns the clause that speaks of the procession of the Holy Spirit: "and in the Holy Spirit . . . who proceeds from the Father [*and the Son*]. . . ." Eastern Orthodox Churches rejected

"West," such that any prospect that true unity in terms of doctrine and polity will one day be achieved among the churches remains dim at best. Why is this so?

People have advanced any number of reasons. One of the most important is the fact that most Orthodox Christians are thoroughly comfortable with their own tradition as it has been preserved and transmitted throughout the centuries. Indeed, they love, honor and cherish it as *Holy* Tradition. Accordingly, they believe that any unity that might be achieved with other churches will necessarily involve unwanted compromise in matters of faith, worship and overall church life. Despite jurisdictional and other internal problems the Orthodox face, they instinctively feel that anything "other" than what they know, practice and love will inevitably mean something "less."

Then again, the pluralism and moral degeneration so prevalent in Western societies today creates among many Orthodox a certain bunker mentality that spills over into the ecumenical sphere. If in some quarters "ecumenism" is regarded as the rankest of heresies, it is because of an understandable, if somewhat paranoid, sense that even engaging in dialogue—not to mention "praying with the heretics"—can only corrupt what they cherish as the treasure of Orthodox Christianity.

There is another reason, however, more fundamental and subtler than either of the above. It is the fact that Orthodox and

---

the addition because it posits the Father and the Son together as sources of the Spirit, thereby undermining traditional trinitarian theology. Traditional doctrine holds the Father to be the eternally "ungenerated" source, who eternally "generates" the Son and "processes" the Spirit. The three Persons share a common divine nature or essence, yet within the Trinity there is a hierarchical order: Father, Son and Spirit, who are equal and undivided. The effect of the *filioque* is to subordinate the Spirit by depicting Him as proceeding from both the Father and the Son as equal principles, thus compromising the identity of the Father as the Monarch or *archē*, the unique principle of all things, both created and uncreated. The recently concluded agreement situates the "coming forth" of the Spirit from both the Father and the Son within the sphere of the divine economy (God *ad extra*) rather than within the being of the Trinity itself (God *ad intra*). This conforms to Jesus' teaching on the Spirit in John 14–16, and it recalls the image of St Irenaeus of Lyon, who spoke of the Son and the Spirit as "the two hands of the Father" (*Against Heresies*, ca. 188).

Western Christians hold very different and basically incompatible worldviews. Let me illustrate what I mean by referring to the domain of biblical interpretation.

Orthodox Christians intuitively identify with the Church's patristic tradition. They consciously strive to adopt the "mind" of the ancient Fathers. Whether they are "cradle" Orthodox or converts, they develop—through liturgical worship as much as through study of the Scriptures—a perspective on reality that is fundamentally at odds with the secularist, postmodern influences of our present day that so strongly shape Western culture, including Western interpretation of the Bible. As we noted earlier, Protestant and, increasingly, Catholic exegesis generally adopts a historical-critical approach, one that finds meaning almost exclusively in the literal or historical sense of the biblical text. (This unilateral focus is attenuated, but not significantly altered, by recent approaches known globally as the "new literary criticism.") The literal sense, once again, refers to the meaning the author himself understood and attempted to convey by his writing.

The Church Fathers, on the other hand, had as their ultimate quest the "spiritual" sense of the text, that is, the meaning that *God*, working through the Holy Spirit, reveals to the Church and world in every successive generation. They attempted to discover this higher, fuller or more spiritual sense by various interpretive methods, particularly allegory and typology. Yet they did so with the conviction that the spiritual sense flows out of the literal sense. Exegesis, therefore, properly begins with investigation of the latter, in order to discern the higher or fuller meaning the Spirit seeks to convey in and through the biblical text.

This movement from the literal to the spiritual sense was possible, in the vision (*theōria*) of the Fathers, because earthly realities in the framework of salvation history are essentially symbolic. In their understanding, events, institutions, persons and rituals of the Old Covenant are prophetic images of future or transcendent realities. To take the most well-known examples: the Exodus served as an image of liberation from slavery to sin and death, and the

Promised Land of Israel was seen as an image of Paradise; Hebrew sacrificial rites prefigured the Church's eucharistic liturgy; and Abraham's willingness to offer up his beloved son Isaac foreshadowed the Father's gift of His beloved Son on the Cross. These types or prophetic images were interpreted in the larger framework of *allegory*. In a word, this means that behind and beyond the literal meaning of the biblical text there lies a deeper meaning that concerns the spiritual and moral life of believers in their quest for salvation. The Fathers took the notion of symbol seriously, since a symbol enables one actually to participate in the reality to which it points. Biblical symbols serve to unite the believer with the transcendent reality that underlies them. Thus, there is a continuum of significance from the manna in the desert to the Church's Eucharist, and on to the heavenly Banquet. A similar continuum leads from animal sacrifice in the Hebrew temple, through Christ's death on the Cross, to the "crucifixion" of oneself—of one's passions and sinful disposition—in the ascetic effort that leads to God-given holiness and eternal life.

While this may sound "Platonic" to most modern ears, it is lived experience for an Orthodox Christian. In the Church's Liturgy we re-actualize and relive the saving events of ancient Israel's history, as we do the events of Christ's passion, death and resurrection. The biblical witness, in other words, is not simply a record of past events that informs our faith. It promotes a living experience, in which past and future are telescoped into the present moment (and therefore in the Church's *anamnesis,* or liturgical memorial, we commemorate or "remember" even what has not yet occurred: the second and glorious coming of Christ!). Scripture, in this perspective, always points beyond itself; and its interpretation within the Church—through preaching and celebration—serves to lead the faithful beyond historical reality and into the realm of the "spiritual," into communion with the transcendent God.

To the Orthodox mind, God is "everywhere present, filling all things." Through historical events and circumstances, He ceaselessly guides His people beyond their ephemeral, earthly life, and into the beauty and joy of His kingdom. There, and there only, lies ultimate reality. And there, too, lies the fulfillment of human life that gives ultimate meaning to an otherwise meaningless existence. Everything in Orthodox experience is oriented toward that transcendent goal: the Church's worship, its interpretation of Scripture, even its acts of charity. It is an experience that creates in the Orthodox mind and spirit what the apostle Paul calls "the hope of glory."

Until our Western partners in the ecumenical debate come to terms with the fact that Orthodoxy lives and breathes in this transcendent atmosphere, that it finds ultimate truth and reality in and yet beyond the bounds of time and space, that it grounds its very life in the immediate experience of the presence, power and majesty of the Living God, then we will continue to engage in a dialogue of the deaf.

Of course, many Western Christians of all traditions share much of this same perspective and same experience. Nevertheless, for the Orthodox allegory and typology remain essential methods for understanding the Scriptures, because they succeed most adequately in revealing and representing a transcendent realm of being in and through the biblical text itself as it interprets events of history. Most Protestants and many Catholics, on the other hand, reject allegory and typology as "pre-critical" and basically useless. This difference in approach to biblical interpretation is symptomatic of the fact that we indeed hold very different worldviews. Western culture, and the forms of biblical interpretation it has spawned, is characteristically secular and dualistic. Just as it tends to separate body and soul, it also separates and compartmentalizes transcendence and immanence, the eternal and the historical. As a result, eyes of faith in Western traditions often perceive God not as intimately and universally present, but as breaking in to creation, into the midst of the historical order, at discrete temporal moments, in order to work His "mighty acts."

As Mary Ford has noted, this secular perspective that separates the sacred from the profane, eternal reality from historical contingency, is responsible for (and reinforced by) a dualistic Christology that is incapable of grasping the reality of two natures, divine and human, fully united in a single Person, Jesus Christ.[6] In extreme forms, this incapacity leads Western theologians to see no ontological relationship whatsoever between the eternal Word of God and the man Jesus of Nazareth. Jesus is reduced in this perspective to the human vessel in which God's Word came to expression. He is no longer seen as the God-man, the eternal Word truly incarnate in human flesh. Secularism, then, is characterized not so much by a denial of God's existence as by a tendency to relegate God to a realm "out there," beyond time and space, beyond the sphere of our daily experience, where He is no longer *with us*.

To the patristic mind, no such dichotomy exists. This explains why the Fathers could envision time and space as charged with eternity, filled with the grandeur of God. It explains as well why their approach to Scripture is so different from the approach taken by post-Enlightenment historical-criticism. To recall an insight of Frances Young: "A culture which can conceive of the material universe as interpenetrated by another reality, which is transcendent and spiritual, will read the reference of scripture in those terms. This is far more significant for the differences between ancient and modern exegesis than any supposed 'method'."[7]

The transcendent worldview of the ancient Church Fathers may seem outmoded and naïve to many people today, not least of all to Western Christian exegetes. To Orthodox Christians, however, the Scriptures themselves locate ultimate truth—and therefore ultimate reality—within the sphere of God's own being rather than within the realm of historical event. Interpretation of the Scriptures, together with the whole of the Church's liturgical life, enable the faithful to experience that reality in the here and now, while they confirm the conviction that the true meaning and

---

[6]See her important article, "Towards the Restoration of Allegory: Christology, Epistemology and Narrative Structure," *St Vladimir's Theological Quarterly* 34.2–3 (1990): 161–195.

[7]*Biblical Exegesis and the Formation of Christian Culture* (Cambridge, 1997), 139.

destiny of human existence lies elsewhere, in the kingdom of "righteousness, peace and joy in the Holy Spirit" (Rom 14:17). In the course of ecumenical dialogue, our Orthodox language and demeanor reflect this experience and this conviction. Where this experience and conviction are not shared by others, there is, sad to say, little chance for mutual understanding, and even less for eventual unity.

6
The Usefulness of Allegory

OST STUDENTS OF THE BIBLE TODAY would consider allegory to be less than useful. In fact they would judge it to be a fanciful, even dangerous way to interpret passages of Scripture. By "allegory," they understand basically what the editors of the *Webster's Collegiate Dictionary* understood: "the expression by means of symbolic fictional figures and actions of truths or generalizations about human experience." For example, Homer's epics are to be interpreted allegorically, taking persons and events as symbols (in the weak sense of the term) or simple metaphors that refer to various acts and experiences we ourselves know, such as our personal "odyssey" through the storms of daily life or the value of courage and heroism.

As it was developed by the early Church Fathers, allegory took up and expanded an ancient approach to the Hebrew Scriptures identified especially with the Hellenistic Jew Philo of Alexandria. To recapitulate the main points from the last chapter: the allegorical approach to interpretation sought to discern in the figures, events and rituals of the Old Testament a hidden reference to similar realities of the New Testament that fulfilled those earlier images. While the Fathers placed different emphases on the historical value of any given Old Testament passage, they were united in their tendency to look beyond its purely historical significance, in order to discover the deeper, higher or fuller meaning that God Himself, acting through the Holy Spirit, wished to convey. (If you are saying to yourself, "this is typology, not allegory," it is important to understand that typology is in fact an aspect or function of the larger interpretive process of allegory.)

Today, most biblical scholars reject the allegorical approach as arbitrary. They cite examples from the ancient patristic writers where the sense of the biblical text is clearly deformed, usually in the interests of drawing from it some lesson to be applied to the Christian's moral life. The Cross and Resurrection of Christ, for example, were seen by some not so much as the means by which our redemption from sin and death is achieved, but as an image of the struggle of the human soul or heart against demonic influence. Without question, the allegorical approach led frequently to exaggerations and outright distortions.

Nevertheless, it is worthwhile recalling that Jesus Himself occasionally used allegory to make a point (e.g., the "sign of Jonah" as an image of His burial and resurrection; His parables), and that virtually every interpreter and preacher of the gospel does the same, whether they recognize it or not. Whenever we attempt to translate a biblical passage into a message for today—to hear the Word that God is speaking to us now, through the text itself—then we are resorting in some degree to "allegory."

An example from the patristic tradition, chosen at random, will illustrate this point and indicate the continuing usefulness of allegory in our efforts to preach and teach the Scriptures.

The theologian Peter of Damaskos (ca. twelfth century) composed many works that are included in the collection of spiritual writings known as the *Philokalia*. In "the Fourth Stage of Contemplation,"[8] he quotes Jesus' words from Luke 17:21, which speak of the presence of the kingdom. The Revised Standard Version translates this as: "nor will they say, 'Lo, here it is!' or 'There!' for behold, the kingdom of God is in the midst of you." The expression "in the

---

[8] *The Philokalia*, vol. 3 (trans. and ed. by G.E.H. Palmer, Ph. Sherrard and K. Ware [London: Faber and Faber, 1984], 126).

midst" or "among you" renders the Greek term *entos*. Depending on the context, however, this word can mean either "among" or "within." Most interpreters today note that from the beginning of His ministry Jesus spoke of the kingdom of God as "drawing near" and being present in His very person. Where Jesus is, there is the realm, or, better, the reign of God. God is present and acting through the person of His Son, with or among Jesus' followers. Therefore they render *entos* as "among you" or "in your midst."

This may in fact be the "literal" meaning of the passage: the meaning St Luke wanted to express (although the more natural reading of the Greek term is indeed "within"). According to this reading, Jesus affirms that the reign of divine power has already dawned, and those who follow Him can perceive the awaited kingdom in His person and therefore "in their midst." In any case, St Luke's primary focus in this passage is on Jesus and the kingdom.

St Peter of Damaskos, on the other hand, attempts to draw from this passage another more "spiritual" (one might say, more existential) meaning for his readers. With most of the Church Fathers, he interprets *entos* as "within you," affirming that the presence and power of God are realized within the inner life of the believer, to guide the believer toward holiness and salvation.

"What can be simpler," he asks, "than giving a glass of cold water or a piece of bread, or than refraining from one's own desires and petty thoughts. Yet through such things the kingdom of heaven is offered to us, by the grace of Him who said: 'Behold, the kingdom of heaven [sic] is within you.' For, as St John of Damaskos says, the kingdom of heaven is not far away, not outside us, but within us. Simply choose to overcome the passions, and you will possess it within you because you live in accordance with the will of God."

In a manner typical of the Church Fathers, Peter passes from the original, "literal" or historical sense of the passage, to a more "spiritual" sense, one that applies to the growth in faith and sanctity of the individual believer. There are two dangers with this approach. First, it risks obscuring the communal, ecclesial framework in which Jesus' teachings need to be placed, by stressing the significance of the passage for each individual Christian. Second, and more important, it shifts the focus from the primary meaning given to these words by Jesus and the evangelist, and places it almost exclusively on the believer's moral and spiritual development.

Some such shift, however, is inevitable when we attempt to draw from the text a message for our time. The Bible, once again, is not simply a historical record of past events. Its proclamation (and celebration) creates a personal encounter between the Word of God and us. That Word is none other than the person of Jesus Christ. To read, proclaim and celebrate His Word, then, is the God-given means by which, through the grace and power of the Spirit working within the Church, words of antiquity become a living witness for today.

As with all things in Orthodoxy, equilibrium—a just balance—is essential. This is especially true in the realm of biblical interpretation. We begin with the gospel witness and make every attempt to discern, accurately and faithfully, the original meaning of a given passage. Yet we move beyond that literal sense, in order to hear and to be nourished by the Living Word who speaks to us today through the biblical text, to realize not only "among" us, but within the very depths of our being, the presence and power of the heavenly kingdom.

7

"But Some Doubted . . ."

THE LIVING TRADITION OF Orthodox Christianity teaches us that nothing is fortuitous, nothing occurs by chance. God is present and acting at every moment and through all things, in order to guide human life and the whole of creation toward fulfillment of His will. This means that He takes upon Himself our struggles and pain, just as He bestows upon us our hope and our joy. In some mysterious way, He also shares in our doubt.

In the biblical accounts, profound meaning is often expressed by small, easily overlooked details. One of the most striking of those details appears at the close of St Matthew's Gospel. In obedience to Christ's command, the disciples leave Jerusalem and come to an unnamed mountain in Galilee. The evangelist continues: "And when they saw Him," the risen Christ, "they worshipped Him. But some doubted."

The other Gospels also bear witness to the doubt experienced by some of those who encountered either the empty tomb or the risen Lord. St Mark's Gospel seems originally to have ended with 16:8. Here the women disciples flee from the tomb with "trembling and astonishment . . . ; and they said nothing to anyone, for they were afraid." The tradition contained in Mark's longer ending (16:14) shows Jesus upbraiding the other disciples "for their unbelief and hardness of heart," because they refused to believe the women's testimony once it was delivered to them.

In his resurrection narrative, St Luke attempts to soften the disciples' reaction with a qualification (24:41): "and while they still disbelieved *for joy. . . .*" Their disbelief, nevertheless, was real.

Finally, the evangelist John focuses the disciples' doubt in the person of Thomas (20:27). It was his unbelief that prompted Jesus to show His hands and side as proof of His bodily resurrection. In response, Thomas uttered the Scriptures' most sublime confession: "My Lord and my God!" Yet later on the disciples continued to doubt, as shown by their reaction to Jesus' appearance by the Sea of Tiberius (21:12).

In his homily on the end of Matthew's Gospel, St John Chrysostom makes a significant point regarding the evangelist's candid admission that some of the disciples doubted, even in the presence of the risen Lord. To Chrysostom, this demonstrates the truthfulness of the tradition, and the willingness on the part of each evangelist to speak frankly of the disciples' weaknesses and shortcomings.[9]

Holy Pascha, celebration of Christ's victory over death by the power and glory of His resurrection, most often elicits among Orthodox Christians an unparalleled outpouring of thanksgiving and joy. This response comes to its fullest expression in the Holy Week services, culminating with the midnight paschal office, followed by the Divine Liturgy. Pascha is above all a feast of light and joy, where we embrace each other in mutual forgiveness and reconciliation. It offers a glorious foretaste of the Great Feast, the Everlasting Banquet to come.

Yet with all its brightness and celebration of victory, some doubted then, and some continue to do so even now.

When I look at the poverty of my faith and the paucity of works of love that flow from it, I wonder just how I came to believe in the first place. All it takes is an unpleasant phone call, or too many demands on my time, or simply getting out of the wrong side of bed in the morning, and I find myself in a mild depression. In that

---

[9]*Hom.* 90.2. See *Ancient Christian Commentary on Scripture*, New Testament Ib, (Mt 14–28), ed. M. Simonetti (Downers Grove, Ill.: InterVarsity Press, 2002), 312f.

state I can't pray—no, the truth is, I simply don't want to pray. I just want to be left alone: by family, by friends, by people in the Church, and maybe above all, by God. Then doubt sets in, not as a rational rejection of the object of my belief, but as an escape from myself and my bad mood, my inability to deal adequately with myself or others in a sinful and fallen world. Doubt in those times is a convenience.

There are other moments, though, when doubt takes on a more insidious form. A news report of thousands killed in an earthquake, or of terrorist bombings that wantonly destroy and maim innocent people, or of priests arrested for child molestation: these things sometimes call up a frustrated and angry question, "Why, God?" "Why do you allow it?" As if I could somehow fathom the mystery of God's workings and will, even if they were revealed to me.

But of all these, the worst is when I allow the faith I have been given by God's grace to be shaken by "thoughts," those demonic voices the Fathers knew so well, that whisper into my ear: "Is it really true?" "Isn't it just a story, neatly constructed, wrapped and delivered by those who want to believe, and therefore want us to believe, yet whose assertions are less fact than wishful thinking?"

In those most awful moments, it feels as though the substance of my faith is slipping away, that my mind is betraying me by offering some rationalization I can't logically reject. Then life itself seems to be ebbing away, and with it peace, longing, and any sense of hope. Those are the worst times, and they have the power to destroy.

The thread that up to now has somehow bound me to a modicum of faith, despite myself, is the memory of a few holy people and a few holy things I have been blessed to know and experience. The face, wrinkled and radiant, of an old Russian woman who suffered through the Revolution, lost her family in their own holocaust, and spent decades in exile. An icon that wept tears of myrrh and filled the sacred space of the little parish church with the perfume of heaven. A Slavonic Liturgy sung with such power and grace that the presence of myriad angels and saints became palpable. A gesture of wholly disinterested, sacrificial love that exhausted the giver yet brought new life to the one who received. A little child who, many years ago, brought me to tears with the simple question, "Daddy, does God love me as much as he loves you?"

These are the things that work miracles against my doubt. Like the faith I claim, and so often take for granted, they are pure gift, wholly unmerited.

When I feel God and life and truth slipping away into a fog of doubt, there remains that perilously thin thread of memory: the memory of grace, of goodness and of love. Then, because God is infinitely faithful, and because countless souls before me have known and lived in the truth and joy of Christ's resurrection, I find myself able to make the simple confessional prayer we are all invited to make: "Lord, I believe; help me in my unbelief!"

8
The "Lack" in Christ's Suffering

*I*N HIS LETTER TO THE CHRISTIAN COMMUNITY in Colossae, St Paul makes a startling and, at first glance, troubling assertion. "Now I rejoice in [my] sufferings [endured] for your sake," he declares, "and I complete in my flesh what is lacking in Christ's afflictions for the sake of His Body, which is the Church" (Col 1:24). In what sense can the apostle complete, make up for, or fulfill *what is lacking* in Christ's own afflictions and the suffering they entail?

From the early patristic period down to the present, biblical commentators stress the point that Christ's redemptive work—the work by which He reconciles rebellious people with the God who loves them and seeks them for His own—was wholly achieved by means of His Passion: His suffering and death on the cross. If the eternal Son of God became incarnate as Jesus of Nazareth, He did so primarily to endure suffering and death, then to rise from the tomb as the Vanquisher of death. Through that unique and decisive act, He destroyed the power of death, and with it the power of sin and corruption, thereby opening before us the way that leads to eternal communion with God the Father. As St Paul and the whole of Scripture make clear, that saving, reconciling work is complete and lacks nothing. Christ has accomplished everything necessary for our salvation, without exception. What can the apostle mean, then, when he declares that he completes the "things lacking" [in Greek, *hysterēmata*] in Christ's afflictions?

The answer can be found in St Paul's understanding of the Church as the Body of Christ. In his earlier letters—to the Corinthians (1 Cor 12–14), for example—he uses the image of a body with many interconnected members in reference to local Christian communities. In Colossians, he is more concerned to stress Christ's Lordship over the entire cosmos, as over the living organism which is the *ekklēsia*, the Church universal. Incorporated into Christ through baptism, the Christian lives in intimate communion with Him. So intimate, in fact, that Christ actually dwells within the believer: "It is no longer I who live," Paul affirms, "but Christ who lives in me!" (Gal 2:20). The apostle's own suffering, endured on behalf of the whole Body, thus shares in Christ's sufferings, because of the communion that unites him with the One who is the Head of the Body (Col 1:18).

Yet the question remains: in what sense do Paul's sufferings make up for what is lacking in Christ's own afflictions?

As so often in Christian faith, we need to hold together in this regard two truths that seem incompatible or even contradictory. We can describe this juxtaposition as an antinomy, a truth that defies human logic. On the one hand, we affirm that Christ alone fulfills the Law, suffers crucifixion and rises from death, in order to release us from the power of death. His suffering is complete, whole, perfect. It lacks nothing, and there is absolutely nothing we can "add" to His suffering, nothing we can do or need to do to fulfill what He has accomplished.

On the other hand, in the time of the Church, and in the power of the Holy Spirit, members of Christ's Body must bear their own suffering, in order for the gospel to be proclaimed and witness to be borne throughout the world. This suffering is necessary and inevitable. Because of the mutual indwelling between believers and their Lord, their suffering and affliction participate in His own suffering for the world's redemption. Their suffering, once again, does not in any way accomplish that redemptive work. That is Christ's role; it is His work and His alone. Yet we are called to "work out" our own salvation in fear and trembling (Phil 2:12), by serving as living witnesses to the gospel. In a hostile and very fallen world, that witness will inevitably invite suffering, as we so clearly see from the persecutions borne by Christians in Asia, Africa and throughout the Middle East, as well as from the personal afflictions so many of us have to endure.

Christ's saving work is complete. Yet our communion in Him involves us—necessarily and inevitably—in our own suffering, for His sake and in His name.

This truth has important implications for each of us, and particularly for those who are subject to acute or chronic suffering, whether physical, emotional or spiritual. Over the years I've had ongoing phone conversations with women who were brought up in satanic cults or exposed as children to severe sexual abuse. A man whom I talked to just a week or so ago has been tempted by suicide throughout his life, at least in part because his father was a violent alcoholic who threatened and beat his son when the boy failed to "measure up." A close friend has for years been carrying on his own battle with a debilitating and potentially lethal disease. These people, and countless others like them, bear suffering that defies comprehension. Every day is a struggle to survive. Understandably, they often feel themselves rejected by God, or at least abandoned and forgotten by Him.

Yet each of them is a member of Christ's Body, and each longs to live in intimate communion with Him. Their most arduous struggle is to surrender their suffering every day into God's hands, with the unshakable conviction that their afflictions truly can and do participate in the ongoing afflictions of the Crucified Lord.

We may never be able to formulate this in a way that is theologically convincing and satisfying. But St Paul's words to the Colossians seem to speak very clearly and compassionately to those who live their lives as "innocent sufferers," people who are not responsible for the agony and anguish that so profoundly mark their every day existence. Insofar as they can take that suffering and offer it to Christ—through gritted teeth, yet with faith and love—they can be sure that He welcomes, blesses and uses it in

His own ongoing work for the world's salvation. Their suffering participates in His; they share, in some mysterious but very real way, in His Cross. And in some equally mysterious way, their suffering is necessary, to fill up or complete what is lacking in Christ's own afflictions.

What is lacking in His afflictions, then, is nothing other than the martyrdom of the saints, as well as our personal martyrdom. This is true at least to the degree that we accept our own affliction, not with bitterness and rebellion, but with courage, patience, and the firm conviction that what we suffer has a purpose, an ultimate purpose that one day will become clear. It is a purpose St Paul describes in another of his letters: "For it has been granted to you that for the sake of Christ you should not only believe in Him, but also suffer for His sake" (Phil 1:29).

When, one day, the meaning of that suffering becomes clear, we shall see that what is lacking in Christ's afflictions is precisely our own participation in them. That participation involves taking upon ourselves seemingly unjust and inexplicable pain and anguish—with patience, courage and boundless trust—with the full knowledge that our afflictions can and do complete His own, for our life and for the life of His world.

9
Bible Study Resources

*T*HERE IS A PERSISTENT NOTION among ourselves as well as among others that we Orthodox don't read the Bible, at least not outside of liturgical services. However accurate this may have been in past generations, it is gratifying to note that it is less and less the case today. Increasingly our parishes—perhaps especially but certainly not exclusively small mission communities—hold regular Bible studies, while priests and teachers emphasize ever more the importance of immersing ourselves in the richness, the beauty and the wisdom of the written Word of God.

Much of this revival of interest in Scripture is due to the efforts of a few dedicated people who have recently published compilations of patristic commentary on both the Old and New Testaments, or have produced commentaries of their own. Among many outstanding resources that we could mention, the following may be of particular interest to Orthodox lay people.

Scholars in Greece and Romania have for many years published technical introductions to both Testaments, and Russian biblicists are quickly catching up. In our own country, we should note the series of introductory and interpretive studies by Fr Paul Tarazi, published by St Vladimir's Seminary Press (Crestwood, N.Y.: 1–800–204–2665 or Online: http://www.svspress.com). One of the best general introductions to scriptural themes remains

George Cronk's *The Message of the Bible* (St Vladimir's Seminary Press, 1982). As for individual books of the Bible, St Vladimir's Seminary has published a fine, pastoral commentary, *The Epistle to the Hebrews,* by Archbishop Dmitri Royster. Accessible to those who have no formal biblical training, this work is also valuable for its deeply sacramental presentation of priesthood: the ministry of Christ as High Priest, but also the vocation of those called to exercise their own priestly ministry in Christ's name.

Some recent compilations of patristic commentary are especially useful in guiding any Orthodox study of Scripture. These can be used with profit to complement annotated Bibles such as *The Orthodox Study Bible–New Testament and Psalms* (Nashville, Tenn.: Thomas Nelson, 1993). The most comprehensive is the excellent series, edited by Thomas Oden and currently being published by InterVarsity Press, titled *Ancient Christian Commentary on Scripture.* This collection will eventually include summaries of patristic insight into the entire Old and New Testaments. It is not cheap; but it deserves to be on the shelf of every parish library.

Another series, less formal and still more accessible, is the "Treasury of Blessings Series," published by Pericope Press (Belmont, Calif.: Greek Orthodox Church of the Holy Cross), under the direction of Rev. Peter G. Salmas (office@goholycross.org). Much of the material presented here is derived from the numerous collections of patristic commentary made over the years by Johanna Manley. Her tireless labors in this area have produced the well-known *Bible and the Holy Fathers, The Psalter and the Holy Fathers,* and *Isaiah Through the Ages.* Perhaps less familiar are her publications on the books of Job and Genesis: *Wisdom. Let Us Attend: Job, the Fathers and the Old Testament;* and *The Lament of Eve* (all available through St Vladimir's Seminary Press). The particular value of the "Treasury of Blessings Series," largely drawn from these other works and amplified by some modern commentary, is its format. The commentaries themselves are accompanied by notes and questions, designed to aid the reader in personal or group study. These, too, make the richness of patristic thought readily accessible to those who feel led to peruse the Scriptures through the lens of Holy Tradition.

Reading over these popular patristic resources makes clear once again just why Orthodox Christians have always held the Church Fathers in such reverence. Whether their approach is literalist or allegorical, whether they stress typological relationships between the two Testaments or the spiritual value of a given biblical passage for the life of the reader, these holy elders hold and convey a vision of God that Christian people, including Orthodox, need urgently to recover.

The Fathers beheld the presence, power and purpose of God in every event and every personal encounter, without exception. If they stressed so strongly the unity between the two Testaments, it was to proclaim and illustrate the truth that the entire history of Israel prepared for the coming of Christ. Yet they also perceived Christ, the eternal Son of God, to be already present in that history, guiding the people toward fulfillment of their divine vocation to "prepare the way of the Lord."

This christological emphasis, however, is grounded in the unshakeable conviction, common to the Fathers, that the Triune God is Lord of heaven and earth, that He alone creates and sustains all things (*ta panta*), just as He labors and longs for all things to participate ultimately in His own divine Life.

As the mysteries of black holes (which sing!) and human cells (which remember!) become better understood, it becomes increasingly difficult for us to imagine that the God who reveals Himself in Scripture can be both Creator and Redeemer—both the cause and the sustaining force behind all reality (including hypothesized parallel universes), and the humble, Crucified One, who lays down His life out of love for every creature that bears His divine image. Yet if the Fathers had known what we know today about the immensity of the universe and the complexity of life, they would have had no difficulty reconciling the two: the image and reality of God as, on the one hand, infinite Power and Majesty, and on the other, unbounded Humility and Love.

So the next time we put down the paper and take up the Bible, we would be both blessed and enriched if we read the Scriptures with the "mind" of the Holy Fathers. Thereby we would allow their wisdom and their perspective to illumine our own minds and hearts, "that we may enter upon a spiritual manner of living, both thinking and doing such things as are well pleasing unto" God.[10]

---

[10]Prayer before the reading of the Gospel in the Orthodox Divine Liturgy.

10

The Breadth of Inspiration

USICIANS, POETS OR GRAPHIC ARTISTS will often claim to be "inspired" to produce a particular composition or design. Like the ancient Hebrew prophets, they feel themselves "seized," "filled" or "carried away" by some invading power. A force from beyond themselves takes control of their mental faculties and guides or compels them toward an expression of beauty and truth.

The end product may be something they had previously imagined in inchoate form, or it may be something astonishingly new and unforeseen. A prophet may speak an oracle whose content he doesn't fully understand because its message is addressed to a wider audience. An artist may want to capture and express something beautiful without any clear idea as to how to proceed. Yet at the moment she begins to execute her work, she finds herself filled and motivated by a force that is not her own, to create beyond her capacities, beyond the limits of her natural talents.

Inspiration takes other forms as well. A priest receives a penitent in confession and hears an appeal for help, guidance and consolation that he is incapable of offering. Silently he begs God to speak through him, to provide him with the words and tone of voice he needs to address the penitent's situation with clarity, firmness and compassion. Then, mysteriously, the appropriate words come. The priest replies to the person before him, yet he knows full well that the words he speaks are not his own. Insofar as they correct, heal and bless the penitent, he can only attribute those words to the inspiration of the Holy Spirit.

The Hebrew term *ruach*, like the Greek word *pneuma*, covers an entire range of meanings for which we need several different expressions in English. Those words we usually translate as "spirit" signify most basically "breath," either human or divine. By extrapolation they also designate the "cosmic breath," that is, the "wind" that comes from beyond. We hear its sound but we know not "whence it comes or whither it goes" (Jn 3:8). These are words Jesus uses to describe the Holy Spirit, who, like the wind, is an invisible but palpable and mysterious power, whose origin and purpose remain unfathomable.

We tend to think of inspiration as being limited to the author of a work of art or a book of the Bible. The artist is seized and compelled to create by the muse, or the apostle is moved to express the Word of God under the guidance of the Spirit. "All scripture is inspired by God," St Paul tells his disciple Timothy (1 Tim 3:16). The second letter of Peter (1:20–21) expresses the same thought, but with an important addition: "no prophecy of scripture is a matter of one's own interpretation, because no prophecy ever came by the impulse of man, but men moved by the Holy Spirit spoke from God." Both passages stress the basic thought that God's Word is authoritative and true. Although it is expressed in human language, it is language inspired by God, with its origin in God. The Spirit works in and through the mind and experience of the biblical author, to shape his message in a way that conforms to God's intention to reveal Himself and His purpose through the author's own words. Scripture is thus a work of synergy: it is a cooperative effort by which God conveys His Word through the medium of human thought and speech.

The passage from 2 Peter, however, takes this a crucial step further. Scripture as a whole derives from the inspiration of the Spirit, yet the same is true with all authentic and authoritative *interpretation* of Scripture. The correct reading of prophecy or Scripture is never "a matter of one's own interpretation," but "moved by the Holy Spirit," the prophet utters God's Word and we receive, understand and internalize that Word. As one Protestant scholar has expressed it, "Without the internal testimony of the Spirit, Scripture remains mute in its witness to the truth."[11]

This means that whenever we read Scripture and attempt to understand its deepest meaning, we can reach that understanding only by the inspiration of the Spirit (professional exegetes take note!). For the Spirit works within our own mind and heart just as He did when He first inspired the biblical authors to compose the canonical writings. What distinguishes their interpretation from ours is not inspiration, but authority. (A work is not "more or less inspired," but it is definitely more or less authoritative: the canon is normative and absolutely authoritative; the Church Fathers possess varying degrees of authority; and anyone who proclaims the gospel today shares that same authority but to a lesser degree that depends on the faithfulness with which they express the gospel message. Yet insofar as any of them proclaim God's truth, they are inspired by the Spirit to do so. Without the Spirit there is no genuine interpretation.)

Here as well an indispensable synergy comes into play. Before the Gospel reading at the Divine Liturgy we ask God to illumine our hearts and to open our minds to understand what the Gospel teaches. For that illumination to occur, however, we need to hear both the words of the Scripture reading and those of the priest who interprets those words. (This is why the sermon should always follow immediately upon the Gospel reading and not be relegated to the end of the service. Scripture and its interpretation form an indivisible whole.) The priest, or any other person in the assembly who preaches, should also be open to the inspirational activity of the Spirit. Thereby an essential continuity is maintained from the initial writing of the Scriptures to their proclamation within the Church.

[11] P. J. Achtemeier, *The Inspiration of Scripture* (Philadelphia: Westminster Press, 1980), 138.

As they composed their writings, the New Testament authors in effect interpreted the Old Testament. The New Testament, then, is essentially preaching or exposition, based on God's words and acts among the people of Israel that prophesied and prepared for the coming of Christ. Subsequently, the ancient Fathers of the Church took up, studied and meditated on the writings included in both Testaments, then they produced their own interpretations of those writings in the form of homilies, theological treatises and biblical commentaries. Like the prophets of the Old Covenant and the apostles of the New, the Fathers opened themselves to the ongoing work of the Spirit, seeking His inspiration in order that their preaching might be faithful to God's intention to reveal Himself and to lead believers to salvation. There is, then, total continuity of inspiration from the prophets and apostles, to the Church Fathers, and on to those in each generation who preach God's Word.

Second Peter, however, suggests that inspiration also plays a vital role in our understanding of and response to the proclamation that has come down to us. Inspiration involves not only prophets, apostles, patristic authors and preachers. It also involves each one of us who hears the Word of God and attempts to put it into practice. If we can allow the Word to resonate in our life, if we are to "hear the word of God and keep it" (Lk 11:28), we can do so only by the inspirational power and activity of the Holy Spirit.

Inspiration, then, is an ongoing work of God that involves all of us. To read and truly understand a passage of Scripture, or to hear in depth the words of a sermon, is in fact possible only by virtue of the illumination provided for us by the Holy Spirit. The prophets and apostles were moved by the Spirit to speak the Word of God, and the ancient Fathers were moved by the Spirit to continue the work of interpretation that constitutes patristic tradition. Each time we take up the Scriptures to read for our own enlightenment, or to tell a Bible story to our children, or to proclaim a message of hope to those who need to hear it, we ourselves enter into that same movement of the Spirit.

We open our minds and hearts to understand the Word of God as it comes to us through Scripture, but also through the Liturgy and through the entire range of ascetic practices and charitable acts that make up our daily life in Christ. Then, by the power and guidance of the Spirit, by His internal testimony, we receive the Word of God, we allow ourselves to be transformed by it, and we bear witness to its truth, so that others, by the grace of that same Spirit, might hear and believe.

11

"Whatever He Hears He Will Speak"

A NYONE WHO READS THE NEW TESTAMENT carefully notices the striking differences between the Synoptic Gospels (Matthew, Mark and Luke) and the Gospel of John. If the first three are termed "synoptic," it is because there are close similarities between them that suggest that they represent a stream of tradition very different from the one that lies behind what is often referred to as the Fourth Gospel.

One element that stands out is the difference in tone and content between these two traditions, Synoptic and Johannine, regarding the words of Jesus. These differences have led biblical scholars, especially since the eighteenth-century Enlightenment, to try to determine the *ipsissima verba Jesu*, the words Jesus actually spoke. Countless books and articles have been written to assess the question. Some scholars, like those associated with the "Jesus Seminar," draw extremely skeptical conclusions: Jesus actually uttered practically nothing that is recorded in the Gospels; almost everything from His parables to His condemnation of Pharisaical hypocrisy actually stems from the "post-Easter Church."

We don't want to enter here into this contentious debate. There is one aspect of the matter, though, that might be useful to take up briefly, since it is one that troubles many of our laypeople, and even some of our clergy who have been exposed in seminary to both the good and the less good in historical criticism as applied to the Bible. This is the matter of Jesus' teaching as it is presented by the Gospel of John. If the tone and content of that teaching are indeed very different from what we find in the Synoptics, what explains that difference? And how can we trust the biblical witness if in fact that teaching derives more from the theological reflection of the early Church than it does from Jesus Himself?

To clarify the matter somewhat, it is first necessary to say a word about the way biblical tradition originated. Most readers of the Bible initially assume that all words attributed to Jesus were actually spoken by Him during the course of His earthly ministry. Subsequently, they notice that in fact a saying attributed to Jesus might have one setting in one Gospel and another setting elsewhere. Then again, different Gospels present similar teachings in different forms. When we compare the Synoptics with John's Gospel, we are struck not only by differences in teaching, but even in chronology. In the Synoptics, for example, the cleansing of the Temple occurs at the end of Jesus' ministry, whereas in John it occurs at the beginning (compare Mark 11:15ff and parallels with John 2:13ff). Then again, the Synoptics present the Last Supper as a Passover meal, whereas in the Fourth Gospel it takes place on the eve of Passover, the day of Preparation (Mk 14:12ff and par.; Jn 13:1ff).

These chronological differences cannot be ironed out; the two traditions cannot be harmonized. There was only one Temple cleansing, and Jesus shared the Last Supper with His disciples either on the Day of Preparation or on Passover itself. What explains these differences? Although biblical scholars are not in agreement on the issue, I believe there is a very simple explanation: the author of the Gospel of John (the apostle John or, more likely, one of his disciples working with the apostle's tradition) modified the chronology for theological reasons. By setting the cleansing of the Temple at the beginning of his account, he creates a parallel with the crucifixion of Christ, recounted in chapter 19. John alone relates Jesus' words after the cleansing that prophesy the destruction of the Temple. Jesus associates this with the destruction by crucifixion of His own body, the true Temple or locus of worship. The parallelism between these two passages, John 2 and John 19, is part of an overall structure that characterizes the Gospel as a whole.[12]

John has also modified the date of the Last Supper to make a significant point. According to his chronology, as the Jews are slaughtering the lambs in the Temple in preparation for the Passover meal, Jesus—the true Lamb of God—is being slaughtered on the Cross outside the Holy City of Jerusalem. Chronology, what we consider historical accuracy, in other words, is less important to the Gospel writers than the theological message they wish to convey.

Something similar occurs with regard to Jesus' words as recorded in the two major Gospel traditions, Synoptic and Johannine. John, more than the others, modifies Jesus' teaching. He amplifies it in certain respects, while nevertheless preserving certain elements even more faithfully than did the Synoptic authors (it is well known that some of John's tradition is older and more accurate than that of the other evangelists). The point is not to determine which tradition is most historically accurate, which one most faithfully reports what Jesus really said. The point is to grasp the purpose of the evangelists' modifications and amplifications of the tradition, and—equally important—to understand just how they could justify such changes.

The answer is provided by the Fourth Gospel itself. During the Last Supper, Jesus delivered essential teaching to His disciples, including words about the role within the Christian community to be played by the Holy Spirit, the Spirit of Truth. When the Spirit comes, He declared, "He will guide you into all the truth; for He will not speak on His own authority, but whatever He hears He will speak . . ." (Jn 16:13).

---

[12]This structure, referred to as "chiasmus" or "concentric parallelism," is discussed by Peter Ellis, *The Genius of John* (Collegeville, Minn.: Liturgical Press, 1984) and by John Breck, *The Shape of Biblical Language* (Crestwood, N.Y.: St Vladimir's Seminary Press, 1994).

If the author of John's Gospel felt free to modify both Jesus' teaching and the chronology of the events of His ministry, it is because he knew himself to be guided into "all the truth" by the Spirit of Truth. The Gospels, once again, are not primarily accounts of history (although they are grounded thoroughly in historical events); they are essentially works of *theology*. They were written "that you may believe that Jesus is the Christ, the Son of God, and that believing you may have life in His name" (Jn 20:31).

John may have modified the tradition he received; but the Synoptic authors did so as well, each in his own way. They could do so—in fact they *had* to do so—because they were conscious of being guided by the Spirit into that truth which Jesus incarnated. Ultimately, then, it does not matter whether a word in the New Testament ascribed to Jesus was spoken by Him during His earthly sojourn, or whether it was "spoken" through the Spirit of Truth after the Resurrection and Ascension.

In either case, the evangelists were under the power and authority of the Spirit. Whatever the Spirit "heard" from the Risen Christ, He transmitted to the Church through the evangelists and other witnesses. What the Spirit heard, He spoke. In their hearing of that message, the inspired evangelists were led to convey through their writings the very Word of Jesus Himself.

12
Why Read the Church Fathers?

THE USUAL ANSWER GIVEN to the above question is that the Church Fathers provide us with invaluable spiritual guidance, based on their own faith and experience. They interpret Scripture and other elements of Holy Tradition in such a way as to educate us in the Way that leads to the kingdom of God. And by the witness of their own life, which often ended in actual martyrdom, they offer us a model of the Christ-centered, self-sacrificing love we are all called to emulate.

These are certainly important reasons that make regular reading of patristic sources not only advisable, but also essential. Without the Fathers' guidance and witness, we would find ourselves adrift in the sea of doctrinal confusion and moral ambiguity that characterizes so much of Christian as well as secular culture today.

Yet there's another, equally significant reason for studying the ancient patristic writings. It is to acquire the worldview of the Fathers, which most people today seem to have lost. This includes a way of looking at history as well as physical reality. If biblical literalism poses for many of us as much of a problem as do certain forms of historical criticism, it is because both are predicated on notions of history, and of reality itself, that are misleading if not false. The presupposition behind both "right wing" and "left wing" readings of Scripture is that truth is revealed only through history, and that history is made up only of facts. Historiography—the writing of history (including biblical history)—thus aims to tell us what really happened: it focuses on events that, theoretically at least, are empirically verifiable. If an event or person depicted in a given body of literature could not in principle have been photographed or tape-recorded, then the narrative account of that event is relegated to the category of fiction.

Jesus' parables obviously fall into that category. They were never intended to recount events that actually occurred. Rather, they are stories that use familiar details of everyday life to convey some moral or spiritual message. Since Jesus' miracles, and particularly His resurrection, cannot be verified objectively, the accounts of those events are also generally dismissed as fictitious. Or at best, they are considered to be parabolic: they are seen as mere illustrative stories, told to make a point. Since their details are unrepeatable and thus unverifiable, the argument goes, they fall outside the realm of determinable fact and cannot be taken as historically accurate, that is, as really true.

From the biblical perspective, as in the view of the Holy Fathers, truth cannot be limited to mere fact, to what is historically verifiable. As we stressed at the beginning of this section, we need to recognize that all "history" is a matter of interpretation. Whether we are talking about Caesar's *Commentaries on the Gallic War*, or Churchill's account of World War II, or a lead article in *Newsweek*, what we receive as history is always colored by the author's own perspective. The same is true even of a photograph. As much as it may capture "reality," that reality is always shaped by the photographer's own perspective, aims and interests. A photograph or history book always gives a subjective representation of reality, rather than an objective rendering of what "really is" or "really was." There can be no historiography that is free from interpretation.

Then again, "truth" (*alētheia*, practically synonymous with "reality") is vastly more comprehensive than what falls into the realm of "history." This is evident from modern physics, just as it is in human relationships. Specialists in relativity theory and quantum mechanics explore dimensions of reality whose existence no one would deny. Yet their investigations fall outside the domain of history; they produce results that are scientifically valid yet nevertheless contradictory (a photon cannot be both a particle and a wave, yet it functions like both; parallel lines cannot meet, yet on the macrocosmic scale they do . . .). In the domain of personal relationships, love is objectively "real." Yet it defies any attempt to define or even describe it, other than by the figurative language of poetry. Neither the movement of subatomic particles nor the movement of the amorous heart is, properly speaking, historical.

If St Basil the Great or St Gregory of Nyssa could approach the Genesis creation stories as they did, it is because they discern *in, through* and *beyond* the so-called historical account other levels of meaning. If St Ephrem the Syrian and St Andrew of Crete could interpret persons and events of the Old Testament as images of Paradise and of the human soul, it is because they, too, discern in, through and beyond the biblical text transcendent reality and meaning. If a literal, historical reading of the biblical text is necessary yet inadequate, it is because Scripture is *iconic,* sacramental. It images and gives actual participation in divine reality, as that reality enfolds and transfigures every aspect of our daily life.

One of the most insightful biblical interpreters of our day is Frances Young, a Methodist theologian who taught for many years in a noted British University. Earlier we quoted from her book, *Biblical Exegesis and the Formation of Christian Culture* (Cambridge: Cambridge University Press, 1997). There she speaks about the current secularized worldview that hampers interpreters of the Bible in their attempts to uncover its true message because of the inability of that worldview to perceive transcendent, spiritual reality present and acting within the material universe.

Young notes that a culture "receives" a text in such a way that the meaning of the text is accepted or contested depending on the "plausibility structures" of that culture. Where the plausibility structures of a particular mind-set do not allow for an interpenetration of transcendent, spiritual reality in the material world, then the ultimate criterion for what is true will be factuality: that is, whether the matter in question is objectively real and therefore historically determinable. And the biblical narratives will be considered true to the degree that they can be shown to recount such historical realities accurately.

To acquire the "mind of the Fathers" is to adopt and internalize "structures of plausibility" that see beyond historical facts to the transcendent, divine Presence revealed in and through those facts. The Exodus, like the Exile into Babylon, is grounded in historical occurrence; some such liberation from Egypt actually happened. If it became the founding myth—the powerful, saving metaphor— of Israel's identity and spiritual destiny, it is because God was at work through that occurrence, but also through its *interpretation* in Israel's sacred literature. The same may be said for the Incarnation and Resurrection of Christ, which we affirm without qualification to be historical events. Yet for those events to have meaning for us—to work their saving power in our lives—they must first be *interpreted* for us by the biblical authors, and then *received* by us in faith. Our worldview must be marked by a profound plausibility, a bedrock conviction that the material universe is indeed interpenetrated by another reality, a reality that is God—transcendent divine Life—who is present and active in every aspect of material reality, with the aim of leading us through this world and into His eternal embrace.

Why read the writings of the Holy Fathers? Because those venerable elders perceived what each of us needs and longs to perceive. Firmly anchored in history, their spiritual vision enabled them to open the eyes of mind and soul to the beauty and glory of divine Reality, as it reveals itself and makes itself accessible in and through Scripture and Tradition, as well as in and through the most mundane aspects of our daily existence.

The Fathers were not more objective than biblical scholars and theologians are today. They, too, gave subjective interpretations to events in the writings they have passed on to us. What makes their witness so unique and so valuable is their capacity to perceive, precisely in and through historical reality, the actual—the utterly real—presence of the living, loving and life-giving God. They beheld, encountered, worshiped and served God in the fallen material world, in the very midst of everyday life. And they invite us to do the same.

II
Contemporary Ethical Challenges

1

In the Hands of God

*L*IFE IN CHRIST IS MADE UP OF countless small yet touchingly beautiful miracles.

Throughout the afternoon I had been reading some recent reflections by a variety of bioethicists on the possibilities and apprehensions surrounding human cloning: in particular, fabricating children in our own image and likeness by asexual replication through the process of nuclear transfer. If the science exists, the specialists argue, why not use it?

Since I had to come up with an answer for the next day's class at the St Sergius Institute in Paris, where I teach for a couple of months each year, I was scrambling somewhat to articulate just why the consensus among Orthodox, and many other Christians today, is so opposed to any procedure whose intention is to take reproduction out of the hands of God—which means to eliminate as much as possible the element of "chance" in the fertilization process—and to offer to potential parents the child of their choice. That is, an offspring whose basic characteristics are determined by the desires of those who will welcome and raise that child to the age of independence. If the parents are going to sacrifice their time, energy and financial resources in such an effort, it seems only reasonable, some people argue, that the child who so benefits should be free of inherited disabilities and endowed with qualities that will conform to the parents' wishes and expectations. And potentially at least, cloning and other forms of genetic engineering offer just such an opportunity to provide "the child we want."

Footsteps resounded up the ancient stairwell. There was a knock at the door, and I opened to welcome our younger son, who is at the Institute working on a graduate degree in theology. After I had stuffed books and papers into a briefcase and we chatted for a while, we decided to go out for some "Chinese." We found the small restaurant we were looking for tucked away on the rue Jean-Jaurès. It was just after six, and since Parisians rarely begin supper before eight, the place was deserted. We ordered a few things, went to a back table and sat down. Once the server set our rice, glazed chicken and other good things in front of us, we began to eat and to talk. The conversation went to his studies and the motivation behind his coming back to Paris, where he was chiefly raised and still feels very much at home.

I listened to him as he talked enthusiastically about projects, plans and hopes. We mused on our respective vocations: priesthood in my case, music and theology in his. He got up and came back with a couple of egg rolls, and we talked some more.

As I listened to this person whom I have known and loved for over thirty four years now, I found myself looking at him across the table with an unaccustomed attentiveness, aware more of his expressions and attitude—what the French call "le regard"—than of his actual words. There was a brightness in his eyes as he spoke of friends, of past experiences and of hopes for the near and distant future. The images his words evoked took both of us to a level of communication beyond conversation.

In that quiet atmosphere we shared a rare and precious moment of communion, in which he became my teacher and I his disciple. In a totally simple, unpretentious way, he talked about his spiritual convictions and doubts, about the silliness of so much that goes on in the Church and its boundless blessings, and about the beauty of liturgical music as a vehicle to attain, here and now, access to the splendor and joy of the kingdom of heaven.

I was, for a while, overtaken with it all: his eyes, his voice, his expressions; his delight with small things in life, together with its often unbearable frustrations and suffering; the spiritual depth of his simple reflections, coupled with a penetrating wisdom regarding my own foibles and misgivings. And I was touched to the point of awe with his willingness to be my friend, to offer me laughter, insight and love.

After we gave each other a bear hug at the metro station and he smiled at me with a warmth that nearly brought tears (I was leaving in two days and wouldn't see him again for several months), he disappeared down into the bowels of Paris, and I wandered slowly back to St Sergius.

Could I ever have selected characteristics and qualities like his in a genetic supermarket? Or had the genius to choose and shape his "traits" into what they were when he was conceived, so that he would become the person he is now? The very question is absurd.

As I climbed those same creaking wooden stairs to my room at the Institute, I realized maybe more than I ever had before, that this son of mine is a pure, unmerited gift. That for some reason I shall never in this world understand, my wife and I have been immeasurably blessed by his smile, his perspicacity, his warmth and affection.

He is who he is, by the grace of God.

I gave thanks for that as I closed the door behind me. And I knew then just what I would try to convey to my students when I met them in class again the next afternoon.

2
The Larger Question

SOME QUESTIONS NEVER GO AWAY, even those we think we've answered once and for all. One of those questions concerns the beginning of human life: when we as human beings actually come into existence. This is a biological issue, intimately linked to, yet independent of, the philosophical or theological matter of when the child *in utero* can be judged to be a "person."

Any number of answers have been given to the question of when life begins. Alternatives are at fertilization, with formation of the one-cell zygote; at implantation, when the developing embryo attaches to the uterine wall and undergoes a thoroughgoing change known as gastrulation or organogenesis; at quickening, when the mother first feels the child move in her womb; at birth, as the newborn infant gulps his or her first lungful of air; or at some later date, once the child has proven itself free of genetic and other disabilities and can lead a "productive" life.

Only the first two of these deserve to be taken seriously.

Christians of all traditions are divided over whether animation is immediate or delayed: whether the embryo is ensouled from fertilization, or whether it becomes ensouled (and hence truly human, truly personal) only with implantation. Orthodox Christians tend to favor the former view; many Roman Catholics and Protestants hold the latter.

At the end of a talk I gave recently on the manipulation of embryos, a woman approached me and identified herself as a Catholic bioethicist who had worked for many years in the field of embryology. In her view, the embryo prior to implantation is properly thought of as a "pre-embryo," since it is characterized by two conditions that are lost with implantation. First, the individual cells or blastomeres are "totipotent"; that is, each one contains the full complement of DNA—the entire, unique genome—and is potentially able to grow independently into a living being. Second, there is a huge percentage of "wastage" among pre-implantation embryos. Between 55% and 75% of all embryos are expelled spontaneously from the mother's body, without her ever knowing she was pregnant. These "mini-miscarriages," coupled with the phenomenon of "totipotency," lead many, if not most people today to regard the pre-implantation embryo as (in this bioethicist's terms) a "substratum" of human existence, but not as actual human life. It is the essential *precondition* for the development of human life, she argued, but it is wrong to confuse it with an individual human being as such, particularly since twinning can occur during the pre-implantation period.

This understanding, I had to admit, is based on a reasonable assessment of the facts. A significant transformation in embryonic life does in fact occur with implantation and the appearance of the "primitive streak" or body axis that will form the central nervous system. From this point on, twinning is no longer possible, cellular totipotency is lost, and "wastage" is reduced to occasional miscarriages.

If this theory of delayed animation is accurate, then we should have little or no ethical objection to the manipulation of embryos, created for purposes of *in vitro* fertilization (IVF) or stem cell research. Presently there are hundreds of thousands of embryos throughout the world that have been produced this way. In IVF procedures, these spare embryos are usually frozen for future use, or given over to scientific research. Some are donated to couples who, for various reasons, cannot produce their own. If these embryos are not human beings, it is argued, then why not use their stem cells for medical purposes, even if harvesting those cells means the embryo dies?

There are many reasons why most people today want to consider the so-called "pre-embryo" to be less than human: a mere substratum of human life, but not life itself. On the one hand, it allows unfettered research on embryos for reproductive and therapeutic purposes, including cloning. It also allows victims of rape and incest to take whatever measures might be necessary to guard against pregnancy, with no moral consequences (that is, expelling a "pre-embryo" would not count as an abortion).

The crucial question, however, is whether there in fact *is* such thing as a "pre-embryo." Can we reasonably argue that the epigenetic information received by the embryo at implantation is so important to its development that prior to that point the newly conceived "entity" does not qualify as truly human? Or is the need for a maternal womb so fundamental in human development that prior to implantation the "conceptus" (*in utero* or *in vitro*) must be considered to be only *potentially* human, hence a "pre-embryo" rather than an individual human being? To answer in the affirmative implies that the newly conceived being has little ontological and no "personal" value in its own right, apart from its integration into the mother's womb. It means that embryos created in a Petri dish have no claim to recognition as "human beings" (and a fortiori as "persons") unless and until they are successfully transferred to a maternal uterus. This is the position represented by recently enacted French legislation that would deny full human status and commensurate legal protection to any embryo that was not the object of a "parental project," an express desire on the part of the parents to bring the child to term and to raise it as their own.

Most Orthodox Christians, together with pro-life people in general, reject the notion of delayed animation and hold that human life begins with fertilization. I have argued for this position in the past and remain convinced that it is correct: that full human existence—both genetic and developmental individuality—is given with syngamy, the fusion of the nuclei of the parental gametes. From this perspective, the very notion of a "pre-embryo" is a chimera, a fantasy invented by proponents of the theory of delayed animation and fervently supported by the pharmaceuticals industry and other commercial interests because of the potential profits and other benefits that would accrue from the harvesting of embryonic stem cells.

On the other hand, by defending immediate animation we set up a major obstacle to research that might lead to the development of medicines and other therapies that could potentially cure neurological and related diseases (Parkinson's, Alzheimer's, and so forth[1]). Even though adult stem cells hold extraordinary potential, embryonic stem cells are easier and cheaper to harvest. Does God call us to oppose this potentially life-saving and life-enhancing research? Or is our opposition simply a replay of the Church's response to the Copernican revolution: a well-meaning but misinformed and misguided reaction against what science has discovered about the way God governs the universe?

From both a theological and a scientific point of view, the real question is not: "When does human life begin?" The gametes themselves are alive; thus the question is a false one, since it implies that there is no "life" prior to the fusion of the nuclei of sperm and ovum. Human life is a continuum, from generation to generation, from the creation of the First Adam until the coming again of the Last Adam.

The question we really need to address is this: "At what point in the continuum that leads from the union of gametes, through implantation and gastrulation, does God bestow on the biological entity we call the embryo the physiological and moral status of human being? Is it at fertilization or at implantation?" This is the decidedly larger question. It is another way of asking just when God endows this new creation with the Divine Image, which implies "personhood."

---

[1]Many specialists have pointed out, nevertheless, that Alzheimer's disease is a complex pathology for which embryonic stem cells have little therapeutic value.

With this in mind, Orthodox theologians and medical professionals need to explore, together and in depth, both the theological and biological implications of the two theories, immediate and
delayed animation, in an effort to determine just which one corresponds most closely to reality. And they need to do so in concert
with specialists in molecular biology, embryology and fetal development. For although most Orthodox Christians hold to the former theory, there are among us highly qualified scientists who are
convinced, on the grounds of their own careful research, that an
embryo *in vitro*, or *in utero* prior to implantation, possesses an
ontological and moral status less than that of a fully human being
or person, even while they grant that such an embryo is fully
deserving of respect and certain legal protections.

That is, we need to explore together what God is disclosing to
us today concerning the mystery of life itself, particularly at its initial stage. In a world marred by terrorism, poverty and a general
disregard for the sacredness of human life, as well as by widespread but potentially curable disease, there is hardly a more
urgent question.

3

The Status of the Unborn—Again

T THE END OF EACH JANUARY we commemorate "Sanctity of Life" Sunday and focus our attention on the tragic number of abortions in the United States and elsewhere throughout the world. It's a time when we again recoil from the realization that the highest abortion rates, as far as we know, occur in "Orthodox" countries. It seems appropriate, then, to consider once more the "status of the unborn," and prevailing attitudes in our own country that permit and even encourage the destruction of the not-yet-born.

When the House of Representatives approved the "fetal protection bill" on April 26, 2001, the non-voting Democratic representative from the nation's capital, Eleanor Holmes Norton, was reported by MSN News as calling the bill "clearly unconstitutional." She specified the reason for her judgment as follows: the bill "defines the fetus as a person in direct, in-your-face violation of *Roe v. Wade.*" That piece of legislation, crafted by the late Justice Harry Blackmun, claimed that "the word 'person' as used in the Fourteenth Amendment, does not include the unborn."

In a similar denunciation of the fetal protection bill, NARAL (the National Abortion Rights and Reproductive Action League), joined by Planned Parenthood and other pro-choice groups, declared that the legislation would give the fetus rights "separate and equal to those of a woman and worthy of legal protection. . . ."

As clearly as *Roe v. Wade* itself, the fetal protection bill forced us to consider once again the status, both legal and moral, of the unborn human from conception to birth. Ostensibly, the bill aimed only to make it a crime to harm or to kill the fetus of a pregnant woman during a violent offense committed against her person. (It did nothing to impose legal limits on abortion, which also kills a child in the womb.) The perpetrator of the violence could be charged with two separate crimes, one against the woman herself, and a second against the child she is carrying. In effect, this legislation simply laid out in modern terms what the ancient Israelites accepted as law over three thousand years ago: "When men strive together, and hurt a woman with child, so that there is a miscarriage, and yet no harm follows, the one who hurt her shall be fined . . . If any harm follows, then you shall give life for life, eye for eye, tooth for tooth" (Exodus 21:22f).

Scholars do not agree on who exactly receives the harm in this passage. One reading understands the child to be dead because of the miscarriage, so concern is only for the woman. In this case, it could be argued that the fetus has no legal status. Another reading holds that the passage speaks of an act that leads to premature birth, and that the harm in question refers to the child. If this reading is correct, the unborn child is recognized implicitly as being fully human and worthy of legal protection.

In any case, the Septuagint or Greek translation of the Old Testament, dating from the third century B.C., clearly understands the object of harm to be the unborn child. A distinction is made between a "formed" and an "unformed" fetus. If the child is born in an "unformed" state, the person who struck the blow must pay a fine determined by the woman's husband. If the child is formed, however, the offender will suffer damages equivalent to those suffered by the child, including death.

According to Israelite law, then, provoking the fatal miscarriage of a near full-term fetus merits the death penalty. This ancient legislation is part of the Book of the Covenant that has shaped Jewish and Christian moral perspectives to the present day. Israel's moral vision was transformed and elevated by Christ, who in the Sermon on the Mount (Mt 5–7) and elsewhere called for a "greater righteousness" than that of the Pharisees. Yet Christ's New Law stands in full continuity with the Law of Moses.

Science and politics often mix no better than oil and water. Although embryology may confirm that human life exists both genetically and developmentally from conception, concern to placate pro-choice advocates has led all three branches of government to preserve the "right" even to such late-term procedures as "partial birth abortion," an act of undisguised barbarity.

While many abortion opponents are trying to overturn *Roe v. Wade* and similar legislation, working as it were from the bottom up, it may prove more effective to reverse course and begin with the most egregious practices in the abortion business. President Bush has expressed clear opposition to partial birth abortions. If they could be outlawed throughout the country, then this would go a long way toward confirming what Jewish and Christian traditions have always known: that life in the womb is human life, worthy of legal protection. Then it would be necessary to work incrementally backward, eventually to eradicate from the public's mind the false distinction between "child," "fetus" and "embryo."

Science operates on the basis of knowledge; politics, on the basis of pressure. It is up to each of us, in appropriate and peaceful yet firm and relentless ways, to apply that pressure. Then eventually we may make it beyond this tragic moment in our history, marked by a level of self-interest that allows incipient human life to be sacrificed in the interests of cloning, the harvesting of embryonic stem cells, and partial birth infanticide. Then finally we might acknowledge and affirm, through public policy as much as through religious conviction, that the "status of the embryo" is none other than the status we enjoy ourselves, as citizens endowed with certain inalienable rights, and as persons endowed with the Image of God.

4
Fetal Farms

*E*VEN IF BIOLOGISTS DO SUCCEED one day in convincing us that an embryo must be implanted in the womb to be fully human, from implantation onward there can be no doubt that the growing life constitutes a *child* : a human being and a bearer of the divine Image. As such, that child constitutes a *person*, who deserves full legal protection against any and all attempts to end its life. Once again, it is God, and not social convention, who determines "personhood," which we can also speak of as "ensoulment." That quality does not appear spontaneously at some point along the continuum that leads from the womb to the grave and beyond. It is bestowed with the act of creation itself.

This, of course, is a theological statement. It expresses a conviction that is foreign to the thinking of major segments of our population. That conviction is nevertheless based on reason and experience. Reason tells us that for life to develop, it must be guided at every stage of its existence not merely by potentiality, but by what it is in actuality. A three-year old is not "potentially" the person he will be at the age of sixty. At three or at sixty, he is the same person, one and the same ensouled being. Similarly, a child in the embryonic stage is not "potentially" the child she will be once she is born. At the earliest stages of her existence she is the very same *person* she will be at birth or on her deathbed. This is confirmed by experience. A child growing in the womb kicks, turns and eventually sucks its thumb. From very early in the pregnancy, the mother "knows" the one growing within her, as a personal relationship with her child gradually takes shape. And that relationship—with its ups and downs, its joys and its sufferings—continues throughout the lifetimes of both mother and child.

From conception onward (whether we identify conception with fertilization or see it complete only with implantation) the child in the womb is a unique, living being, an actual and not merely a potential person, by virtue of the fact that it does indeed bear the Image of its Creator. That theological conviction, though, is hardly shared by those whose vision of human life is shaped by a secular worldview that easily banishes God from the arena of daily affairs when His presence threatens to frustrate utilitarian ends.

A recent development, noted but barely discussed by the media, illustrates as clearly as any other the slipperiness of the moral slope on which we now find ourselves. This is the sanctioning by certain local governments of so-called "fetal farms," biomedical companies that will produce human lives with the intention of destroying them before birth for utilitarian purposes.

In a world that has tossed away its moral compass, there's a simple and sure way to get what you want. When your initial demand is rejected, increase the demand tenfold, and they'll give you at least what you originally asked for, and maybe a good deal more.

The abortion and pharmaceutical industries, together with other vested interests, initially demanded that "extra embryos" from IVF procedures be used as a source for stem cells. This provoked moral outrage in some quarters, so they shrewdly upped the ante. They pressured the New Jersey legislature at the end of 2003, to pass Assembly Bill 2840, a measure likely to have more far-reaching consequences than *Roe v. Wade*. The bill not only legalized the cloning of human embryos. It allowed those embryos to be implanted into a woman's uterus, grown nearly to term, and then aborted before birth, in order that their various body tissues and organs might be used for "therapeutic" ends.

Increase the demand exponentially, and they'll give you in any case what you originally asked for, and maybe more. Keep working this model, and eventually what was considered outrageous yesterday will seem reasonable today.

Opposition to the request for legalizing use of embryonic stem cells, in other words, moved those who would most profit from such use to make a still more outrageous demand: that babies be created, carried in the womb until the ninth month of gestation, then—by legal edict—killed. If this egregious violation of everything from human dignity to human rights is accepted in New Jersey, it will not be long before it is accepted throughout the country. "Fetal farms" will spring up, where not-quite-born-yet children will be destroyed for purposes of experimentation and organ harvesting. And yesterday's opposition to embryonic stem cell research will "melt like wax before the fire."

Miscarriages, as tragic as they may be to the parents who experience them, are morally neutral, the unintended consequence of biological vagaries in a fallen world. Fetal farms, however, which will exist with the express intent to create and then destroy living human beings, are the epitome of moral depredation. Now only an impending threat, they may soon become reality. Like pornography or addictive drugs, with time they will elicit increased tolerance. And with it will come an increased cheapening of human life.

Just a couple of years ago we were sweating out the moral implications of destroying embryos in order to obtain their stem cells. Today we are envisioning the creation of fetal farms where children will be conceived, grown in the womb, and then intentionally killed for allegedly therapeutic purposes. We have become inured to the whole issue, though, because for so long we have tolerated such practices as "partial birth abortion," a euphemism for an act that in reality is nothing short of murder.

Certain powerful elements in our society have successfully disguised their greed as a commitment to promote advancements in the field of medicine. Not long ago, they persuaded us of the need to create embryos by *in vitro* fertilization. Next, they convinced us of the advantages in destroying those embryos to produce various medical therapies. Most recently, the New Jersey legislature and like-minded people have upped the ante. Now they are asking not only for embryos to kill, but also for fetuses to extract, dissect and distribute.

"Increase the demand outrageously," they said to themselves, "and they'll give us what we originally asked for, and maybe more." Now we're on the verge of giving them fetal farms. What will it be next time?

5
"Goodbye, Dolly!"

NEARLY A DECADE AGO, the world said "hello" to Dolly, the first mammal to be asexually produced through a process of cloning. On February 14, 2003, scientists at the Scottish Roslin Institute, where Dolly was created and lived, announced that they had to euthanize Dolly, because she had acquired a progressive and fatal lung disease.

In its report on Dolly's death, the Associated Press declared that her case "raised questions about the practicality of copying life." It concluded by noting that many other animals have been cloned (pigs, cows, ponies, goats, mice, cats, and most recently, a dog), and added: "many of them appear . . . robust and healthy." To the mind of the London based AP reporter, this last point apparently reduces the matter to one of "the practicality of copying life." He gave no hint that there might be a moral question involved.

CNN, on the other hand, reminded its readers that already in 1999, researchers had determined that Dolly's DNA was in effect the same age as the ewe from which she was cloned. The so-called telomeres, or natural endings of the chromosomes contained in the nuclei of the clone's cells, were shorter than normal, indicating premature ageing. Extrapolating on the case of Dolly, one specialist in human genetics and cloning, Dr Patrick Dixon, was quoted as saying: "The greatest worry many scientists have is that human clones—even if they don't have monstrous abnormalities in the womb—will need hip replacements in their teenage years and perhaps develop senile dementia by their twentieth birthday."

As could be expected, spokespersons for the Roslin Institute claimed that Dolly actually succumbed to a viral infection caught from other sheep housed with her. They concluded that it is "unlikely" that her illness was due to her being a clone.

However that may be, the likelihood that the cloning process itself is inherently flawed raises the most serious objections to its use as a means to reproduce human embryos. Yet with the media focused so heavily on the continuing war in Iraq and on natural disasters throughout the world, laboratories in the U.S. and in many other countries are proceeding apace, with little or no public oversight, to reproduce human embryos with the purpose of harvesting their stem cells or implanting them in the womb of a surrogate mother.

The problem with "copying life"— animal or human—is not one of "practicality." It is the most significant and troublesome moral issue of our age, even considering the AIDS and Ebola epidemics sweeping across Africa, and the increasing breakdown of the nuclear family in a great many Western nations.

There is little chance we will be able to mobilize massive street demonstrations against cloning, as anti-war activists have recently done in opposition to our presence and policies in the Middle East. The issue is too little understood and the consequences too little appreciated by most of the world's population, including our own.

This makes it all the more imperative that the churches—individual parishes and bodies such as SCOBA—work to inform their faithful of the true significance and threat of human cloning, and urge them and the general public to pursue every appropriate means to bring to a halt the international movement to legalize the practice, whatever justification for it may be offered.

In the United States this means not only prohibiting the use of public monies to support cloning and the embryo manipulation that underlies it. It means passing legislation to outlaw the procedure altogether. Otherwise, Dolly's fate may well befall coming generations of our own children.[2]

The dictionary notes that the expression "goodbye" or "goodby" entered the English language sometime in the mid-sixteenth century, as an abbreviated version of "God be with you." With Dolly's premature demise, and the increasing threat that cloning poses to human as well as animal life, we would do well to return to the original sense of that expression. As we say goodbye to Dolly, may we pray that God will be with us, to make effective and lasting our efforts to insure the integrity and well-being of human life at every stage of its existence, even from its very beginning.

[2]Europeans find it incomprehensible, and basically hypocritical, that the American public bans use of public funds for reproductive cloning yet accepts unquestioningly the "right" of private industry to manipulate and destroy embryos as it pleases, with no legal consequences.

6

Medically Assisted Procreation: Second Thoughts

NOT LONG AGO, THE AMERICAN PRESS REPORTED, with a combination of shock and amusement, some fantastic developments Italian scientists had achieved in the domain of procreative medicine. Given the relative ease with which embryos can be created these days *in vitro*, Italian specialists in the field of MAP (medically assisted procreation) were enabling post-menopausal women to become pregnant, pregnancies to occur on a routine basis using donor sperm and ova, and grandmothers to carry *in utero* their own grandchildren and bring them to term. The floodgates had been lifted up, and what walked in was anything but glorious.

The reigning mentality was not unlike what we find today in France. There embryos are considered to have no ultimate value or dignity unless they are part of a *projet parental*, an express plan and desire on the part of the parents to give birth to those embryos. If no such *projet* exists, then the embryos, created in the laboratory, are fair game for research purposes, including the harvesting of stem cells, which naturally destroys them. This same reasoning lies behind popular support for "IVG"— *interruption volontaire de grossesse*—what we call abortion on demand. (Although the French, like members of the European Union in general, place a limit to the practice at twelve weeks—and regard "partial birth abortion" as an appalling act of barbarism).

One of the most outspoken pro-life groups in France, which vehemently opposes this kind of manipulation on both scientific and theological grounds, is the *Fondation Jérôme Lejeune*. Lejeune was a world-renowned embryologist, who made headlines with his discovery of the cause of Down's Syndrome. He showed that the disability is a result of "trisomy 21," an anomalous condition in which there appear three rather than the normal two twenty-first chromosomes. Lejeune has been vilified by everyone from atheists to Orthodox in France because of his *intégrist* tendencies: the perception that he was an inveterate and irredeemable apologist for the Roman Magisterium, at least in matters concerning abortion and embryo manipulation.

Nevertheless, the Foundation that carries on his work publishes a very useful monthly newsletter that addresses, as few other organisms in Western Europe dare to do, critical issues concerning human life at all its stages of development. A recent letter gave a summary of Italian legislation, the "Law of 19 February 2004," which was published on February 24, 2004 in *Gazetta Ufficiale*. The legislation is titled "Rules concerning medically assisted procreation," and it speaks directly to the anarchy that increasingly reigned in Italian medical facilities.

In reaction to growing trends, the Italian government set out guidelines for all forms of medically assisted procreation. MAP is legally available only to a couple constituted of a man and a woman, both of whom are living. (This is in response to recent pregnancies produced by insemination using the sperm of deceased donors.) MAP must also be "homologous" rather than "heterologous": that is, the gametes must be those of the parental couple, thus excluding donor ova and sperm; and the child must be brought to term by the biological mother, thus excluding recourse to a "surrogate mother."

Furthermore, strict measures have been included to protect human embryos. They may not be created, by fertilization or cloning, for research purposes, nor may their genetic material be manipulated for eugenic purposes. "Designer babies," consequently, are out. Moreover, any medical team that adventures into the realm of human cloning exposes its members to a punishment of ten to twenty years of prison time, together with a fine of 600,000 to one million euros (multiply that by about 1.25, and you see what it means in dollars).

With regard to *in vitro* fertilization, which has become so routine in the U.S. that hardly anyone questions the practice today, the Italian law is equally clear. In a word: no "extra embryos." All embryos created *in vitro* must be implanted immediately, which limits their number to about three. By contrast, consider that in the United States today (this is a guess, but it's too low, if anything) there are some 400,000 frozen embryos, left over as a result of IVF procedures, the vast majority of which will be used for research or simply discarded.

If human life in fact begins at fertilization, as Orthodox tradition holds, then we can only applaud the initiative of the Italian government in setting such clearly defined limits to MAP. No matter who is sitting in the White House, chances of similar legislation in this country are—given the popular mindset—simply nil. Perhaps the Italians have become more aware than we have to the dangers of promoting a "culture of death." If so, it would be in large measure because of the relentless struggle waged by Pope John Paul II against the abusive manipulation and destruction of human life at every stage of its existence.

If the Pope can speak out as clearly, courageously and firmly as he has, can we hope for the same from our own Orthodox bishops, theologians and medical professionals? If Italy can step back from the abyss of moral anarchy in matters of medically assisted procreation, is there any chance that we can do the same?

7
"Whose Body Is It, Anyway?"

SINCE THE U.S. SENATE IN 2003 voted overwhelmingly to ban the late-term procedure known as "partial birth abortion," we have been led, as Christians in a highly secular and pluralistic society, to look once again at the implications of what the French euphemistically call the "voluntary interruption of a pregnancy."

Over the centuries, theologians have held divergent views regarding the beginning of human life and the point after conception at which a "person" can be said to exist. We noted above that some Church Fathers hold to "immediate animation," while others opt for a theory of "delayed animation." To the former, fertilization and conception are synonymous, and they understand that human life, even "personal existence," begins with the creation of the genetically unique zygote, the single-cell embryo at its earliest stage of development. The latter group argues, on various grounds, that the soul only "enters" the body at some point after fertilization—for example, at implantation or quickening—and only at that point do they consider the process of conception to be complete.

Given our knowledge of embryology today, there can be no doubt that the embryo is a genetically unique organism from the time at which it is formed by the fusion of the nuclei of sperm and ovum. The gamete of each parent normally contributes twenty-three chromosomes, producing a new human being with a unique composition of forty-six chromosomes, arranged in pairs. Since the chromosomes contain the body's DNA, the "genetic blueprint," the embryo is without question a living, genetically unique organism from *fertilization,* one that will, if left to develop normally, grow in an unbroken continuum through the various stages we (misleadingly) label zygote, pre-embryo, embryo, fetus, and newborn infant. To emphasize once again what should be self-evident: from one end to the other of that continuum, it is a matter of a living, growing *child.*

What needs to be stressed is the *uniqueness* of that child from the very beginning, a uniqueness that is both genetic and developmental. To move from embryological to biblical categories, this means that from conception the child growing in the mother's womb is a living human being: a composition of flesh, soul and spirit that constitutes the somatic unity the apostle Paul speaks of as the "physical body" (1 Cor 15:44). Because that child is created in the Image of God, he or she is also a *personal* being, with a specific and unique origin and destiny.

A classic rebuttal to pro-life militants is the ironic, rhetorical question that has been raised as often as any other in the thirty odd years since *Roe v. Wade.* "Whose body is it, anyway?!" The question presupposes that a child growing in the mother's womb, at any stage of the pregnancy from fertilization to birth, is little more than a mass of tissue, comparable to a mole, a fingernail or a strand of hair. Accordingly, the answer to the question can only be: "Well of course, it's yours!" There is only one body involved worthy of consideration, it is argued, and that belongs to the woman who finds herself pregnant.

If the "growth" were anything other than what it in fact is—a unique, living human being—then the woman would have every right, both moral and legal, to dispose of it as she wishes. The fact is, however, that the child's uniqueness—again both genetic and developmental, growing in a continuum from conception toward birth—means that it is definitely not analogous to some bodily growth. It is a unique and complete human being (as "complete" at its own stage of development as a two-year old or an eighty-year old is at his). Therefore, it possesses the moral quality—and should be accorded the same legal protection—as any newborn infant or adult.

Because this truth has been formally denied by our country's laws, it has been obscured in our collective conscience. The logical and inevitable result has been 1.3 million convenience abortions each year, several thousand of which have been "partial birth." This means that several thousand of those abortions have involved legally sanctioned infanticide.

Abortion kills a living human being. This is as true at the embryonic stage as it is at later stages of growth in the womb, including the moment of birth. To deny this is to deny the witness of God's Word as well as the givens of modern embryology. And indirectly it is also to deny the seriousness of "post-abortion syndrome" that so often weighs upon mothers (and fathers) who have opted to terminate a pregnancy.

Whether we like it or not, sexual activity carries with it very definite responsibilities. If a woman is subjected to the violence of rape or incest, any resulting pregnancy has a very different moral weight than it does in cases where she engaged freely in the act that resulted in conception, even though such violence in no way lessens the full humanity of the child growing within her. In any pregnancy, the mother's responsibility extends from herself—from her own body—to the life and body of the child she is carrying.

To raise the issue of responsibility today, especially in the realm of sexuality, is to offend political correctness in the most flagrant way. Nevertheless, we need more than ever before to educate, with love and clarity, the children who are ours—both boys and girls—if we are to help them to assume a truly responsible attitude toward sexuality and its consequences.

Whose body is it? It's the woman's body *and* that of her baby. It's the father's body *and* that of the child he helped conceive. Each of these bodies, in the final analysis, belongs to God, who creates us in His image, animates us with His life-giving Spirit, and calls us, from conception to death, to grow into His perfect likeness.

8

Torture in the Womb

ORTURE EVOKES FOR MOST OF US feelings of dread, anger and loathing, responses based at least in part on the fear that it could happen to us or to someone dear to us. Because of today's headlines, the word "torture" itself calls up images of an Abu Ghraib prison, or the beheading of a Nick Berg, or the "necklacing" of some unnamed victim of Africa's internecine wars. For some people the term brings back acutely painful memories of childhood abuse at the hands of a demented parent or a sinister satanic cult.

There is another form of torture, sanctioned by this country's legislation, which receives far less attention, because to speak of it is politically incorrect. Yet it is the most widespread form of torture used in this country, and it needs to be recognized and named for what it is. I'm speaking about the torture associated with various forms of mid- to late-term abortions.

More than thirty years ago, Justice Harry Blackmun of the U.S. Supreme Court declared: "the word person as used in the 14th Amendment does not include the unborn." This opinion, enshrined as law by *Roe v. Wade*, greatly facilitated the rush toward convenience abortions by the subtle message it conveyed. If a "fetus" (as distinct from a "child") is not a "person," then presumably that fetus is devoid of personal characteristics, including the capacity to feel pain.

Pro-life people tried to sensitize the public to the truth of the matter by a variety of means, such as the film "The Silent Scream," and graphic descriptions of saline abortions. It was to little or no avail. The American public has accepted convenience abortions as a normal feature of its cultural life, including the procedure known as partial birth abortion. As we all must know by now, this involves rotating the pre-born, full-term infant; drawing the body, feet first, out of the birth canal so that only a portion of the head remains "unborn"; then stabbing the back of the child's head to make an opening, so that the brain can be vacuumed out and the skull crushed. In this way thousands of babies are killed each year, although reputable witnesses, including the American College of Obstetricians and Gynecologists, have declared that there is never any medical need for such procedures. It is nothing other than a legally sanctioned means to rid oneself of an unwanted child. In other words, legally sanctioned infanticide.

At the beginning of June 2004, the media reported the decision of U.S. District Court Judge Phyllis Hamilton, holding that the congressional ban on partial birth abortions was unconstitutional. She argued, against prevailing medical opinion, that there is no clear evidence that a child experiences pain as a result of the procedure. And she added that the question of pain is "irrelevant," presumably because the laws allowing it give no consideration to the issue of pain, but focus entirely on the rights of the mother to end the life of the child growing within her.

One pro-life media source, (*www.lifenews.com*) noted what could only be regarded as an appalling irony: "Hamilton said the issue of fetal pain is also not germane because unborn children may feel greater pain in other abortion procedures such as 'disarticulation abortions'—where the baby is dismembered."

Does a newborn infant feel pain? Does a child in the womb feel pain? The answer should be self-evident, if for no other reason than the fact that a pregnant woman often feels the child's reaction to her own stress. And the monitoring of children who are being aborted, at least in later stages of the pregnancy, shows undeniably that they experience acute pain throughout the procedure, that is, until they are dead. Imagine yourself (or your child) being torn literally limb from limb, until some vital organ is destroyed and the agony finally ends.

This is ugly stuff, I realize. It is bound to provoke a hostile response on the part of pro-choice people and some bitter anguish on the part of women who have undergone an abortion. I very much regret adding any distress to the many women who are suffering what is known as "post-abortion syndrome." And I readily acknowledge that there are times when a woman simply cannot bring a conceived child to term, when her only recourse is to abort. (As has often been remarked, many pro-choice women in fact have no real choice whatever in deciding to end their pregnancy.)

But for too long we have kept silent about this entire question. During the past three years or so, pro-life concern has focused almost entirely on embryos, primarily because of the dispute over harvesting embryonic stem cells for therapeutic purposes. Embryonic life is certainly human life, and it needs to be respected and protected to the fullest extent. Yet the nervous system is not integrated before about the eighth week after fertilization. This means that the embryo feels no pain.

This is not the case with a developing fetus: a child growing in the womb.[3] The principle of protecting embryonic life must unquestionably be preserved and defended. But every bit as important is protection extended to a sentient being, in this case a child who can feel pain, who can fully experience the consequences of being torn apart or having scissors thrust into the back of his or her skull.

The moral standing of a society is measured by the way it treats its most vulnerable members, particularly the very young and the

[3]Researchers are very much divided on the question of just when a child in the womb is actually capable of feeling pain. Some place it at 20–24 weeks, others much earlier. Most acknowledge the obvious: that victims of partial birth abortion experience acute pain, even if they may process it differently than would, for example, a two-year old. Only recently has the suspicion been confirmed that young male children also feel pain while they are being circumcised.

very old. If American society considers the pain suffered by a child during an abortion to be irrelevant, then we have sunk to the level of barbarism. It may be irrelevant given the laws we allow on the books, and it may be irrelevant to those who profit most from the abortion industry. But it cannot be considered irrelevant by anyone with a moral conscience.

It is time, then, that we broaden our perspective and speak out loudly and clearly to legislators, medical professionals and others who shape public opinion. It's time we look reality in the face, acknowledge what we are doing to 1.3 million unborn children each year, and—while we beg God's forgiveness and healing for our moral blindness—work in our parishes, in our homes, through pro-life organizations and in our legislatures, to end what has rightly been called the "abortion holocaust." It's time we hear the Gospel command to offer our "little ones" to Christ: not as victimized cadavers, but as living, prosperous, secure and cherished bearers of His divine image.

9
Care for Patients in PVS

O N MARCH 20, 2004, POPE JOHN PAUL II addressed a gathering of physicians and theologians on the issue of care for patients in a chronic condition known as a "persistent vegetative state" (PVS). This is a condition, often referred to as "brain death," brought on by severe and irreversible damage to the cerebral hemispheres. It leaves the patient with no capacity for self-awareness or ability to relate to others. Since the lower brain is intact, however, autonomic and motor reflexes function normally. The patient experiences ordinary sleep-wake cycles and often emits sounds that can be misunderstood as attempts to speak. Nevertheless, their brain is effectively dead except for the brainstem (which controls breathing and heart rate) and perhaps portions of the limbic system (body temperature, blood pressure, blood levels of sugar). Where this so-called vegetative state has persisted for more than a few months, there are no documented cases of full recovery. (The term "vegetative" refers to the condition; it does not imply that the patient is less than human or is no longer a "person" in the full sense of that term.)

The Pope was responding, at least in part, to the much-publicized case of Terri Schiavo, a PVS patient whose husband long sought to have her feeding tube removed. He finally succeeded, leaving her to die of dehydration in March of 2005. Although she had been diagnosed as being in a "vegetative" state, this was never clearly demonstrated. Where there is doubt, as in this case, nutrition and hydration should definitely be continued. In cases where the patient is actually in PVS, removal of nutrition and hydration leads quickly to death, usually in just a few days. Many ethicists argue that such removal is morally acceptable, since the underlying cause of death is the irreversible medical condition that prevents the patient from taking food normally.

Since the early 1980s it has been clinically established that withholding food and hydration from terminally ill patients—that is, those who are actively engaged in the dying process—can be beneficial. It allows the buildup of nitrogen wastes that produce azotemia, a natural analgesic, and can enable the patient to slip into a coma and die peacefully. On the other hand, continuing to provide food and water through intubation in terminal cases can increase the patient's sense of pain and suffering, without offering a proportional benefit.

The question raised by the Schiavo case, as by the Pope's declaration, is whether it is ever morally and medically appropriate to remove food and hydration from a patient in PVS. Such patients are not, in the strict sense, terminally ill; that is, they are not actually dying, even where there is no chance for recovery. Provided with food and water, they can live for months or even years. Yet their physical existence is preserved only by life-support technology, and they remain in a state of permanent unconsciousness. If that technology were not available, such patients would quickly die, since they are incapable of feeding themselves or of being fed orally.

Catholic moral theologians have long debated whether providing nutrition and hydration to patients in PVS falls into the area of "ordinary" or "extraordinary" means. If the former, then such treatment is ethically mandatory; if the latter, then, weighing burdens against benefits, it may be morally appropriate to withdraw all life-support and allow the patient to die. Pope John Paul II's declaration made it clear that he located the providing of food and water

in the realm of ordinary means, and therefore it is morally obligatory in cases of PVS. Many Catholic ethicists, however, feel otherwise. They argue that there comes a point in a person's life
where administering artificial nutrition and hydration merely hinders the patient from attaining what we request in our Orthodox
prayers: a "peaceful separation of soul and body," "a painless,
blameless and peaceful" end to earthly life and the passing on of
the person to the ultimate end of human existence, which is eternal communion with God in the kingdom of heaven.

In light of those prayers and the Orthodox perspective on the
mystery of death, we need to have as our primary concern the best
interests of the patient. No one wants to lose a beloved friend or
family member. Accordingly, there is a strong temptation (and
often pressure) to do "all possible" to ward off death, even if it
means preserving a minimal level of existence by purely artificial
means. We need to ask, though, whether such actions serve the
interests and well-being of the patient, or whether they derive
from our own reluctance to accept the loss associated with death
and to surrender the person into the hands of God.

This raises the question of the "quality" of the patient's life.
Often the decision to provide or withhold nutrition and hydration
is based on a subjective judgment as to whether the patient's existence is worth preserving The issue has unfortunately been polarized between those who argue for "sanctity of life" criteria (life is
inherently sacred, therefore it must be preserved at all costs) and
those who argue for "quality" considerations (if that life is deemed
worthless or pointless, then there is no obligation to preserve it).

This way of raising the question, however, is false and misleading. All human life is inherently sacred, and it is precisely that
sacredness that invests it with its ultimate and indelible quality.
This means, however, "there is a time to live and a time to die."
Death in a biblical perspective—a Paschal perspective—is no
longer "the last enemy." Death itself has been destroyed, and "we
are given Life." From the time of our conception until the end of
our physical existence, the very purpose of our being is to allow

the Holy Spirit to work within us the transformation from a "body of death" to "life in Christ," a life that begins in the present age and endures through and beyond physical death, into the fullness of life in the kingdom of God.

When a person is dying—when "the soul is struggling to leave the body"—then, again, it may be morally permissible, even obligatory, to withhold nutrition and hydration, in order that death may come naturally, as a regretted end but a blessed beginning to a new order of life. Can we say the same of patients in PVS, who, technically, are not terminal?

All we can conclude, it seems, is this. Where there is no chance for recovery other than through God's own miraculous intervention (which can occur at any point), then it seems reasonable to conclude that artificial means of life-support, including nutrition and hydration, may be morally withdrawn or withheld. The final judgment needs to be made not by distinguishing "ordinary" from "extraordinary" means, but by weighing the possibilities for cure. Where further medical intervention is futile, and merely hinders the person in his or her struggle to die, then such intervention should be judged to be abusive rather than beneficial. Medical heroics in such a case are morally inappropriate.

Yet any decision to remove life-support, particularly in nonterminal cases such as PVS, must be taken as the fruit of ardent and disinterested prayer. This does not mean that we should expect that an answer to the question regarding appropriate treatment or nontreatment would be written on the wall. It means that members of the Church community—including the family, friends, and insofar as possible the medical team—offer the patient to God through ceaseless intercession, asking for both clarity and charity in making what could be their final decision regarding that patient's future and well-being.

In the final analysis, everything depends on our motive. Where our primary concern is for the ultimate healing and salvation of the person in question, then we can make decisions, even in a state of uncertainty and confusion, with the confidence that God, in His time and in His way, will indeed work for that person the paschal miracle that leads from a "dying life" through physical death, and into Life beyond.

10
PVS Revisited

I N THE PRECEDING CHAPTER WE RAISED the issue of "Care for Patients in PVS," or "persistent vegetative state." With the storm of controversy that surrounded the case of Terri Schiavo, it seems worthwhile to return to the question of her actual condition, and to ask about terminal care in general.

Terri was diagnosed by her physicians as being in a persistent vegetative state, a diagnosis vehemently disputed by her parents and by other medical specialists. Her estranged husband and legal guardian, Michael Schiavo, repeatedly sought a court order to have her feeding tube removed. Public outrage led Florida Governor Jeb Bush to intervene at Michael's first successful attempt, leading to a reversal of the order and passage of "Terri's Law." Pressures continued, however, to deprive her of food and hydration, and thus to "allow" her to die. Upon her death, her husband (who, following Terri's collapse in 1990, fathered two children by another woman) reportedly stood to collect a large sum of money. Finally, he won out. Despite the valiant efforts of her parents, joined by a great many pro-life advocates from around the country, the tubes were removed and Terri died of dehydration.

The entire issue is a critical one, and its consequences could have a direct impact upon the life—and death—of any one of us. The whole question in Terri's case turned on the diagnosis and definition of PVS. The *Merk Manual of Diagnosis and Therapy* and other medical dictionaries define PVS as a chronic state that results from severe and irreversible damage to the brain hemispheres, such that only the brain stem is adequately functioning. Despite misleading signs of consciousness noted earlier, with patients in PVS there is in fact no cognition, no perception of stimuli, and, after a period of two or three months, no chance for recovery. The person is in fact "brain dead," even if a distinction can be drawn between their actual state and a state of "deep coma."

Every indication is that Terri Schiavo in fact was not in a "persistent vegetative state," as that expression is normally defined. She experienced periods of consciousness and clearly responded to the presence and words of her family members. From photos and films of her behavior that circulated in the media, it was apparent that her smiles and eye contact were more than mere reflex actions. They offered sound evidence that she was to some degree aware of her surroundings and was capable of interacting with other persons and with aspects of her environment.

Nevertheless, the fact that she was often "nonresponsive" led some medical professionals to support her husband's demands that she be dehydrated and left to die. As Wesley Smith has pointed out, "Patients diagnosed as being permanently unconscious— PVS—can almost never be saved from dehydration once the primary caregiver decides to stop tube-supplied sustenance, *even if* close family members object."[4]

Care for seriously disabled patients should be determined by the actual circumstances of the case, rather than by the wishes of those who would benefit from the patient's demise. This should be evident to any disinterested observer. It is necessary, though, to make a crucial distinction between (1) cases of terminal illness, where the patient is engaged in a dying process and "the soul is struggling to leave the body"; and (2) cases of PVS or other conditions (such as Terri Schiavo's) where the patient is not "terminally" ill but can be maintained on life-support.

In the former situation, it may well be appropriate to withhold all life-support, including a nasal-gastric tube, for the reason we have noted before: to allow natural analgesics to build up in the body and ease the patient through the dying process. The diagnosis of "terminal" illness, or a "terminal" condition, however, should not be understood as it so often is: that the patient has "less than six months to live." No one can predict with certainty the condition of a patient over that span of time. "Terminal" should refer to a patient who is clearly and irreversibly dying, a state that can be diagnosed with a high degree of accuracy by medical specialists.

In Terri's case, however, as with many patients who are (mis) diagnosed as being in PVS, the expression "terminal" does not apply. They are not dying. As inconvenient, expensive or burdensome as their care may be, they are living persons who deserve every legal and moral protection we can offer. They deserve to live, rather than to be put out of the way.

If a person is in a critical state because of illness or an accident, then it is essential that the medical team respect a basic rule of thumb: when in doubt, opt for life, whatever the expense, however great the burden. This is our moral responsibility before God and before one another. That rule does not mean that we resort to medical heroics and ignore a "Do Not Resuscitate" (DNR) order or other advance directive (a living will, for example). It means rather that when the wishes of a critically ill patient have not been and cannot be clearly expressed, the medical team will presume that the patient would want life-support measures to continue, until and unless the person actually reaches a terminal state and such measures become burdensome rather than beneficial.

An important means of preparing for that time is for each of us to name a proxy, a friend or relative, who will accept "durable power of attorney" or "power of attorney for health care decisions," in order to see to it that our will regarding treatment will be respected, if we are no longer competent. This is more effective than living wills, which are often misinterpreted, or simply ignored, at the critical moment.[5]

Within our parish communities, as well as among family and friends, we should be able to find such a trusted person. Through their accompaniment and their prayer, that person can assume on our behalf the basic priestly role that consists in offering our life and our condition to Christ, so that our passing from this world to the next might be truly "painless, blameless and peaceful." We should not have to depend, like Terri Schiavo, on public outcry in an attempt to forestall a gross violation of civil rights and an affront to human dignity. As members of the Body of Christ, we owe to one another the degree of care and love that will guarantee that each of us faces death, not with the fear of abandonment to a cruel and untimely death, but with serenity and unshakable hope.

---

[5]As with all those who hold power of attorney, the proxy must be legally appointed. This requires filling out proper forms that are available in most lawyers' offices, in many hospitals, and at the state health care department.

11

Maggie, Terri, and the Problem of Life-Support

THE FILM "MILLION DOLLAR BABY" caused quite a stir in certain pro-life circles. Although director and actor Clint Eastwood dealt with the tragic end of his heroine's life with sensitivity and compassion, many people were shocked at his apparent endorsement of euthanasia. The controversy was unnecessary because the entire problematic surrounding Maggie's death was based on a grave if common misunderstanding.

For those of you who haven't seen the film but might like to, it would be best to stop here until you do.

Eastwood's character, Frankie Dunn, has attended Mass nearly every day for some twenty-three years. Estranged from his own daughter, he befriends then virtually "adopts " Maggie Fitzgerald (Hilary Swank), who plays the Oscar-winning role of a young woman determined to make her way in the brutal world of professional boxing. Following a gratuitous punch she receives after the bell, Maggie is paralyzed, condemned to spend the rest of her days in a bed, and slowly wasting away. For both her and Frankie, this is an unbearable situation that throws into question her very reason for being. Finally, in a gesture of heartrending compassion, Frankie reluctantly gives in to Maggie's repeated appeals and pulls the plug (in fact, he injects a substance—epinephrine?—into her IV line and thereby crosses the crucial line between allowing to die and actively killing). As the film ends, Frankie seems to be spending his remaining days in relative solitude and anguished soul-searching.

The very premise of the film is seriously flawed for the simple reason that throughout the last days of her life, Maggie was conscious and, theoretically, competent to make her own decisions regarding life-support. The film rehearsed the familiar scenario of a person in perpetual agony, desperately longing to die yet prevented from doing so by a medical team that insists on keeping them alive by artificial means (respirator, intubation, antibiotics). A consensus has emerged among most Christian confessions, including Roman Catholic and Orthodox, that "extraordinary means" may be foregone in cases such as Maggie's, if the decision to refuse such measures is made by a competent, well-informed and (clinically) nondepressed patient.[6] Refusal to resort to life-support, when the burdens of those means clearly outweigh the benefits, can also be expressed in a living will and / or by granting some trusted person durable power of attorney for health care decisions. In Maggie's case, the burdens of her care, her level of physical and mental suffering, the material costs involved, and the "futility" of prolonging life-support could justify, to most minds, cessation of that support, in order to allow her to die. This would not qualify as "euthanasia," since the patient would succumb to the underlying pathology. Maintaining life-support, on the other hand, would amount to "medical heroics" that place sustaining biological existence above the desires and interests of the patient.

There are those, of course, who argue that biological life has such inherent value that to remove life-support—even in a case

---

[6]The qualification "clinically" is important here. Anyone in Maggie's condition would be susceptible to depression. In cases of long-term, clinical depression, however, which might be independent of and merely intensified by the patient's present condition, attempts should first be made to provide relief through medication and possibly psychotherapy, before any decision is taken to obey the patient's wishes to be free of life-support. Often it is difficult to distinguish "clinical" from ordinary, occasional, or non-life-threatening depression, and the principle of patient autonomy means that the final decision regarding life-support and related care should be left in the hands of the patient and / or that person's representatives (health care proxy, spouse, parents, and so forth).

such as Maggie's—is immoral, since it bases the decision on "quality of life" rather than "sanctity of life" criteria. This, however, represents a very un-Christian form of "vitalism" and is not an acceptable argument. The entire gospel message teaches us that the true end of our biological existence is precisely to pass through the crisis of death, in order to attain eternal life in the kingdom of God. The longing for such total communion with God does not allow us to hasten our death through some form of suicide or euthanasia. But when we become the victim of an accident or illness to the extent that life is permanently and irreversibly characterized by unbearable suffering, then artificial measures to sustain that life represent a violation of life's *sanctity*, a violation of the person, and may morally be withheld or withdrawn. In those cases where the patient has entered the terminal phase of life (engaged irreversibly in the actual process of dying), then, as noted above, removal of life-support may include not only a ventilator or dialysis machine, but also food and hydration.

This last measure, however—withdrawing food and liquid—can only be morally accepted in cases that are truly "terminal," that is, where the patient has entered the final phase of life and "the soul is struggling to leave the body." This implies that death is imminent and that the dying process is in fact irreversible.

Such was clearly not the case with Terri Schiavo. Films taken of her during her final months of life, the recognition she showed of her family members, and the awareness she demonstrated in response to various external stimuli, made it clear that she was not, as it was held, in a persistent vegetative state. It seems that in her case, as in many others, the term PVS was redefined for political rather than medical reasons. Under these circumstances, for the courts and Terri's guardian (her estranged husband Michael) to force removal of her feeding tube was tantamount to murder: the willful taking of a life against the best interests of the victim.

This conclusion holds, even in light of the autopsy report, whose author declared that Terri was in PVS because her brain "was profoundly atrophied." Medical specialists from Harvard,

Johns Hopkins University and The Cleveland Clinic were quoted as stating that PVS is a clinical diagnosis that cannot be confirmed by autopsy. The autopsy could indeed show that she had suffered from a severe and irreversible brain injury. It could not, however, demonstrate that she died (from dehydration) without acute suffering, or that she had no awareness of the presence and affection of her family members and priest. That priest, Fr Frank Pavone, declared shortly after Terri's death: "No details of this autopsy change the moral evaluation of what happened to Terri. Her physical injuries and disabilities never made her less of a person . . . Terri did not die from an atrophied brain. She died from an atrophy of compassion. . . ."[7]

If Terri had left a living will or given her parents durable power of attorney, the situation would never have arisen. Living wills are often ignored; but health care decisions can be delegated to competent proxies who can confirm that they know the patient's desires regarding end-of-life care.

These two cases, represented by the fictional Maggie and the all-too-real figure of Terri Schiavo, should give us all pause. Pause to recognize how steep the slippery slope has become that is hurtling us toward legalized euthanasia and physician-assisted suicide, but pause, too, regarding the importance of making known to other people—family and friends, our doctor, the clergy, and among them, potential proxies—just what we want for ourselves in the way of life-support measures, should the situation arise.

In a case such as Maggie's, the burden-benefit calculus is morally legitimate, even necessary, so long as any decision to end life-support is made by the person involved or by others designated by the person to act in their stead. There where life can be preserved without rapid and painful deterioration, then

---

[7]A misdiagnosis of PVS can have tragic consequences. See Kate Adamson's book, *Kate's Journey: Triumph over Adversity*, and the report in *The National Catholic Bioethics Quarterly* 5.2 (2005): 232 n.12. Adamson was diagnosed as being in PVS, her feeding tube was removed, yet she recovered eight days later. She reported that during that time, while she was conscious yet unable to communicate, she experienced "sheer torture."

life-support may be considered mandatory, at least from a Christian point of view (the State has no inherent right to force a person to remain on life-support when such support violates the person's autonomy and imposes unbearable suffering). As bearers of God's image, we are called to cherish and preserve our entire life, including our physical existence, as fully and faithfully as we can.

This means that we, as Christian people, may at certain times and in certain circumstances accept levels of ongoing suffering that many in our society would reject on principle. We may do so, however, as long as that suffering is not accepted or sought out for its own sake, as a kind of prideful, self-serving martyrdom. Suffering, especially in terminal cases, can indeed be redemptive. But suffering can also become so burdensome that the person can concentrate on nothing else. In extreme cases it can become impossible to pray or even to relate in any meaningful way to those around us. Pain and anguish can become so all-consuming that physical life itself becomes an intolerable burden. When such levels of suffering occur in clearly terminal cases, then it is not only futile but cruel and unreasonable to maintain the dying patient on life-support. An acceptable protocol would instead include appropriate pain management and measures to assure as much comfort as possible. As anyone who has accompanied the dying knows, it is far better to die in hospice than in an ICU.

Such are the crises we face at the end of life in this age of awesome yet often burdensome technology. We need to face those crises, however, and to do so in communion with others: family, medical professionals and the church community. Dying should never be a solitary, lonely experience. It should be a profoundly ecclesial act, an act transformed into a *sacrament*, by virtue of the unwavering love and compassion of those who accompany us through it. This level of compassionate caring may have redeemed to some degree Maggie's death. The lack of it on the part of the decision makers in Terri's case, however, turned her death into a terrible and irredeemable tragedy.

12

The Healing Power of "Offering"

A YOUNG ORTHODOX PRIEST HAD JUST ARRIVED in the hospital waiting room to minister to a grieving family. He talked for a while with the oldest member, a man in his late sixties who was struggling to come to terms with his wife's rapid decline.

The priest— call him "Father Paul"—spent a few minutes with the husband, then went into the ICU where the dying woman lay semicomatose, a ventilator pumping air into her tired lungs and tubes protruding from her wasted arms. He looked at her for a few moments, took out his prayer book and read several petitions. Finally, he blessed her, anointed her, and asked God to grant a peaceful end to her suffering. Then he returned to the waiting room and tried to comfort any of the family members who seemed open to his ministrations.

When I spoke to him later that day, Fr Paul vented a great deal of frustration over what he felt was his incapacity to minister to this family in any really healing way. He had tried to serve them on many different levels: as a friend, as a grief counselor, and as a witness to God's love. It quickly became clear that his sense of failure was due mainly to the fact that he had not been able to offer either the dying woman or her family members the degree of solace and relief from depression he felt they needed. He concluded that in fact the nurses and the social worker had provided more for the family than he had himself. With a slight edge of bitterness he added, "In seminary, nobody ever taught me how to relieve people's grief." Then he added, "Maybe I just should have gone into counseling."

Behind his reaction there is a great deal of misunderstanding as to the real purpose of priestly ministry. In this therapeutic age it's probably inevitable that we want above all to relieve people of their physical and emotional suffering. Seminary faculty members, whether priests or not, often feel that they have succeeded if a student who comes to talk during office hours leaves feeling better than when he arrived. Then they wonder why, a day later, the student is still depressed.

The same is true with many priests who spend long hours hearing confessions and making hospital visits. Their primary aim is very often to console, to help, to unburden the person before them; in a word, to make them feel better. Then they feel frustrated when the person continues to experience guilt, anxiety, loneliness or grief.

Of course we want to relieve the suffering of others. That effort, too, is part of living the gospel. But it is not the primary aim of priestly ministry.

We need constantly to remind ourselves that the priesthood is a universal vocation. Every baptized member of the Body of Christ is consecrated to "a holy priesthood, to offer spiritual sacrifices acceptable to God through Jesus Christ" (1 Pet 2:5). Some are ordained for a specific function within the Church; they are endowed by grace with the particular responsibility and capacity to celebrate the sacraments. Others in the congregation can assume different functions, such as preaching the Word of God and teaching elements of the faith, even though these as well normally fall to the priest.

The same is true with pastoral care. Because he is salaried by the parish, the people often assume that the priest alone is responsible for ministering to the sick and suffering, by making house calls, visiting people in hospital, and offering comfort to those burdened by grief. Many also assume that the priest, or a selected elder in the parish, is there to provide inexpensive counseling. If this almost inevitably means "cheap" therapy, it is for two reasons. First, because except in special cases, neither priest nor parishioners have been trained to do therapy or to offer proper psychological counseling. More importantly, it is because they have misunderstood the most fundamental purpose of priestly ministry.

It is crucial that we minister to those in need through whatever means may be at our disposal. Pastoral counseling offers valuable opportunities for exercising that ministry. But it remains a secondary function relative to the chief purpose of the priestly vocation, whether ordained or lay.

That purpose, alluded to earlier in our introduction, is to make an *offering* of everyone who seeks and longs for eternal communion with the Holy Trinity. As ordained clergy or as laypeople, each of us is called to offer up the world and one another "to Christ our God." Thereby every moment, every event, together with every life and experience, can participate in the eucharistic elevation: "Thine own of Thine own we offer unto Thee, on behalf of all and for all."

In the case of Fr Paul, this means that his responsibility and his blessed privilege is first of all to pray with and for the dying mother and her loved ones. Through his prayer, which participates in the eternal intercession of the communion of saints, he makes the one gesture that can bring real and lasting healing to each member of the family, including those who die. That gesture consists in offering each of them to God, to His glory and praise, begging that His will be done in each life concerned.

In this way, Fr Paul performs an act, a sacred service, that each of us is called to render, particularly in situations of death and dying. Because each of us will die one day, we all find ourselves in such situations at every moment of our life.

He may not make the family feel any better. He may not be able to alleviate their burden of grief. But if the priest or some other member of the community can make an offering of each family member to God—through his prayer, anointing, comforting, and any other appropriate means—he has done what is essential. He has placed them all into the care of the only true Physician of our souls and bodies, the only One who can truly heal. And thereby he has fulfilled, in the most faithful way possible, his priestly vocation.

III

Throughout the
Liturgical Year

1

"Most Holy Theotokos, Save Us!"

O RTHODOX CHRISTIANS BEGIN AND END the liturgical year with celebrations dedicated to the Virgin Mary, whom we venerate as the *Theotokos* or "bearer of God." On September 8, the end of the first week of the new year, we commemorate her Nativity or birth; on August 15, the year begins to close with the feast of her Dormition, that is, her "falling asleep" and translation to heaven.

As the hymns of these and other Marian feasts make clear, our veneration of Mary, the Mother of God, is basically a confession of our faith in the Person of her Son. All Marian piety, in other words, is an expression of christological dogma. It points beyond the Virgin herself and focuses on the significance—for her as for us—of the One whom she bore in her womb, our Lord Jesus Christ.

In the troparion or festal hymn of her Nativity, we affirm the truth that "the Sun of Righteousness, Christ our God, has shown forth" from her. By virtue of the fact that she gave birth to this One who is both Messiah (Christ) and Lord (God), the "curse" of our sin and resultant condemnation has been annulled. These words are reminiscent of the apostle Paul's declaration to the Colossians: Christ has canceled the legal bond (judgment) that stood against us; He has set it aside, "nailing it to the cross" (2:14). The troparion concludes with the Paschal assurance that this Son of Mary has bestowed upon us the blessing of eternal life by destroying the power of death. As the Author of Life, He has descended into the realm of death; and by His resurrection, He has opened the way for each of us to rise up with Him and to share in His eternal glory. The troparion of Mary's Dormition continues this theme by referring to her as the prototype of all of those who will be translated from death to life at the General Resurrection. The hymn begins by affirming a twofold miracle: although she gave birth in the flesh to the eternal Son of God, she did not lose her virginal quality. Virginity in this sense is above all a sign of purity and holiness, of self-sacrificing love. These virtues Mary preserved fully, even though she experienced pregnancy and the opening of her womb. This wonder is coupled with a second: the fact that her death does not at all separate her from the world, from the human objects of God's boundless love and mercy. Accordingly, she is able constantly to intercede for us before her Son and our God, and thereby to "deliver our souls from death."

Mary in no way replaces her Son in the work of salvation, nor does she serve in the technical sense as "mediatrix" or mediator between God and mankind. Although the liturgy at times attributes to her the title Mediatrix, the expression must be understood in the light of her Son's saving activity. She mediates for us only insofar as she prays and intercedes on our behalf. This is the calling—and the blessed possibility—offered to all of us, insofar as we, like the Mother of God, willingly offer ourselves, together with the world around us, to the mercy and grace of our Lord.

There is only "one Mediator between God and men," the apostle declares, "the man Jesus Christ, who gave Himself as a ransom for all . . ." (1 Tim 2:5f). Orthodox Christians know this intuitively. Yet they also know that Jesus' mother never ceases to intercede for us and, indeed, to mediate our prayer before God.

For this reason, we conclude most of our liturgical services with a word of supplication that to many people, including many other Christians, sounds scandalous or blasphemous: "Most holy Theotokos, save us!"

"How can you Orthodox pray that?" a Baptist friend asked me one day.

If Jesus is truly the eternal Son of God, the God-man who became flesh in the womb of Mary; if in and through her person He, the Second Person of the Holy Trinity, actually assumed our human nature, to transfigure that nature and restore it to its original intended purity and holiness; if His saving, redeeming work was made possible by Mary's *fiat*, her willing acceptance of virginal birth-giving through the power of the Holy Spirit—if all of this is true, then we can do nothing other than acknowledge her role in God's economy of salvation, and celebrate that role, with joy and conviction, in the services of the Church.

If Jesus is truly who we believe and confess Him to be, then we can do nothing other, and nothing less, than exalt His humble mother as truly *Theotokos*: a human person like ourselves, but whose womb "became more spacious than the heavens" by bearing the incarnate Son of God. And if, from her Nativity through her Dormition and beyond, she is truly who we believe and confess her to be—the Mother of God—then we can do nothing other, and nothing less, than ask her to intercede ceaselessly for us, for the sake of our salvation.

The most ancient icon we possess is a fresco of Mary found in the catacombs in Rome. There she offers herself as she does in the familiar image of the Deisis: standing upright, her hands lifted in supplication, making intercession on behalf of us all. She is the Orante, the very incarnation of ceaseless prayer. "The prayer of the Mother has great power to win the favor of the Master," we declare in the office of the Sixth Hour. That eternal fountain of intercession serves as a model for our own prayer, as it makes its appeal to Christ and to His Father on our behalf. This extraordinary promise, that her prayer can serve our salvation, is equally a promise that our own intercession can serve God's work for the salvation of His world.

We address our supplication to her, therefore, asking that she pray for us, that she intercede for us, before her Son and our

God. And we do so in the full knowledge that we can ask the
same of one another and of all those who dwell in the Body of
the risen Lord.

> O Most Sovereign Lady Theotokos, you are more honorable than
> all the angels and all creation, a helper of the wronged, the hope
> of the hopeless . . . the salvation of sinners, the help and protec-
> tion of all Christians. Through your mercy save and have mercy
> on all the faithful. Grant, O Lady, peace and health to your ser-
> vants, and enlighten their minds and hearts unto salvation,
> granting us, your sinful servants, the kingdom of your Son,
> Christ our God.
>
> [From the Akathist to the Most Holy Theotokos]

2
Incarnate Love

URING THE SEASON OF CHRIST'S NATIVITY, the title of Vigen Guroian's fine collection of essays on ethical issues, *Incarnate Love*,[1] comes to mind with special poignancy. Reflections of that love, however—made by those who care for the suffering, the poor, and victims of catastrophe—are not at all limited to particular seasons of the year. Cases in point can be evoked by the simple mention of a date or an event: September 11, 2001; December 26, 2004; Hurricane Katrina . . .

For the past several years I've spent a couple of weeks each spring in Romania, visiting theological faculties, monasteries and parish churches. A recent brief tour of Transylvania made me more aware than ever before of the material deprivation so many Romanian people still face in this post-Communist era. It also made clear the depths of love and commitment with which many of the more privileged Romanians, together with a significant number of Americans and other foreigners, are attempting to meet the needs of the poor, the sick and the marginalized.

Poverty conditions in parts of Eastern Europe, as in the developing countries of Africa, are at times beyond the comprehension of most Americans. One evening the family who was hosting my wife and me drove me into downtown Cluj-Napoca.

[1]First ed.; (Notre Dame, Ind.: University of Notre Dame Press, 1988).

There, in a small religious bookstore, I met a woman in her mid-seventies who earns her meager living translating articles and books for a local Orthodox publisher. Her income does not allow her the luxury of buying the heart medication she needs, although it is relatively inexpensive. Often she does not have enough to eat, simply because she has no money at all. The concept of "disposable income," or even of a bank account, is incomprehensible to her, as it is to many of her compatriots. Yet she is a person of culture and quiet dignity. (She apologized that her French was not as good as it used to be, then in that language she conversed fluently about her situation, but also about French and Romanian literature). She has a son on this side of the ocean, a computer programmer who used to send her money on occasion. His live-in girl friend, though, has forbidden him from doing so any longer, and the mother now receives nothing from him. If she doesn't starve to death, it's only because a few friends offer her what they can out of their own limited means. And hers is hardly an isolated case.

Other situations also tug at heart and conscience. During the Ceaucescu era, government policy outlawed contraception as well as abortion—not for moral reasons, but to increase the population for political and military purposes. Now the country is rife with abandoned and abused children (every month an average of six children are abandoned in the single city of Cluj).

Small but significant efforts are underway, nevertheless, to address this well-publicized and still critical situation. Craig and Victoria Goodwin, for example, working in conjunction with the Orthodox Christian Mission Center in Florida (www.ocmc.org) bought and renovated a large house in a poor section of Cluj. With teams of volunteer workers, they cared over several years for groups of a half-dozen orphans less than two years of age. Under the eves they set aside two rooms for pregnant women who were looking for the support necessary to allow them to bring their child to term rather than resort to an abortion. Under the Goodwin's care the home was spotless and well equipped, and the atmosphere was warm, loving, and compassionate. Even after their departure and return to the States, it remains so today.

Little Angela, about 18 months old at the time, looked up at me with her dark eyes and timid smile. She is part Gypsy and so has little if any chance of being adopted in her native country. Those eyes followed me as I left the house, and we peered at each other through the window. If I could have put her in my pocket and brought her back home with me, I would have. Tragically, though, there's a moratorium on foreign adoptions. The Goodwins devoted themselves to Angela and to the others with tender affection and extraordinary self-sacrifice (although they would not see it that way). I finally left the house and returned to our friend's apartment. For hours that night I lay awake, marveling at little Angela's gaze, but also at the work the Goodwins and their successors have undertaken. A handful of kids, that's all. But it's a gift of life to each of them.

Some thirty years ago I was hunched, terrified, in the back seat of an old French DS, tearing down the Paris-Lyon autoroute at 180 km. per hour. The driver was a hotshot young businessman, who nevertheless lived his Catholic faith with seriousness and a certain sense of joy. We just learned that today he is in Romania, working with orphans.

A close friend in Paris, who many years ago became a nun in the Romanian archdiocese, is making plans with others to create an orphanage in Moldavia, the eastern province of Romania. Once it's completed, they will be welcoming several hundred children and providing them with everything from medical care and education to a quality of family-like love most of them otherwise would never know.

And so it goes. Simple people like ourselves, with no other agenda than to "be Christ" to the poor, the abandoned, the rejects of contemporary society. And just as many stories, of course, could be told of people in this country who work to improve living conditions, education, and medical care for those in poverty, and who do so with incarnate love. That is love which has taken flesh. It is love like the love of Jesus, who spoke a word or touched a wound, and brought healing.

At Christmas time especially, we can only give thanks to God for the gift of that love, as Jesus Himself incarnated it, and as it becomes incarnate through the lives of all those who make of their existence something of a reverse tithe. They live on ten percent of their resources and offer the rest to the less privileged.

May God bless their efforts and strengthen their dedication. May He allow them to touch others with the same healing power He conveyed to Peter's mother-in-law, to the woman with the issue of blood, and to Jairus' deceased daughter. And may He touch our own hearts as well, that we might share in those good works, that we might in our own lives and activity give flesh to that love which knows no bounds.

3

The Eternal Mystery: From Annunciation to Nativity

ONE OF THE MOST PRECIOUS COMPONENTS of Orthodox Christianity, perhaps especially in the Russian tradition, is its store of melodies to liturgical hymns that are heartbreakingly beautiful. I just came across a fine example, tucked away in the iTunes folder of this laptop. It's a contemporary variant of a hymn sung normally at Annunciation, composed by Fr Paul Jannakos. The message it proclaims has special resonance in the Christmas season as well, the time of our Lord's Nativity. The hymn was recorded in the summer, between those feasts, by an impromptu family quartet: simple, no frills, and lovely beyond words. The version they sang was this:

> The eternal mystery is revealed today:
> God the Word of God becomes the Son of Mary the Virgin.
> Gabriel heralds the Annunciation of joy.
> Let us cry with him: Rejoice, O Mother of our God!

At one time or another, most of us become frustrated with what we perceive to be the stultifying inertia or irrational zeal that can seize our clergy, hierarchs and "influential laypeople." We deplore the obstacles thrown up in the way of ecclesial unity and the establishment of a truly local, self-governing Church. Some of us become exasperated over disputes between authorities of our various jurisdictions, or money mismanagement by our bishops and diocesan treasurers, or authoritarian decision making or an absence of decision making, or priest transfers made willy-nilly and not made when they need to be made, or misbehavior on the part of those who should know better. Others among us, with a more highly developed social conscience, complain that we Orthodox spend too much time "liturgizing" and hobnobbing with one another, when the world in its appalling spiritual and material poverty so desperately needs to be fed, clothed, visited and healed.

It would be a shame, though, and even sinful, to forget or underestimate the extraordinary treasure that we so often leave hidden in the field of our tradition. Moreover, we need very much to hold things in perspective. While we squabble about jurisdictions, finances and matters of ecclesial authority—all of which are doubtless serious and important concerns—most of the rest of Christendom is caught up in doctrinal uncertainty and moral ambiguity to the point that increasing numbers are jumping ship from the traditions of their youth. While we debate relatively trivial matters such as what, if any, "secret" prayers are to be said aloud or whether we should raise parish assessments, many people of Christian background are "imaging and imagining" a dual-gendered God, or dismissing as myth the divinity of Christ, or laughing at the Virgin Birth, or militantly defending "reproductive rights" that include infanticide. We are blessed beyond measure by the doctrinal and liturgical unity that we share as Orthodox Christians. Our real sin in the midst of a world of confusion and unbelief would be to leave the treasure of Orthodoxy buried in that field.

From Annunciation to Nativity, we have an exceptional opportunity to proclaim to the world, including to other Christians, that, indeed, the eternal mystery has been revealed: that the eternal Word of God, who is Himself God, has become the Son of Mary, the Virgin, and that He has done so for our sake, out of His inexhaustible love for us and His insatiable desire for our salvation.

In our own life, and in the celebrations of our parish communities, we can step back and relive that mystery to the full. We can celebrate the services of these Feasts, not out of habit or some sense of obligation, but because those services give us access to the mystery as nothing else can. They enfold us in the reality of Christ's incarnation so that we "remember" it in the profound biblical sense of the word: we relive it and share in it. We take that mystery into ourselves, we allow our minds and hearts to be reshaped by it, and gradually we discover it to be the unique and glorious way to liberty and life.

If it is appropriate to recall an Annunciation hymn up to and through the season of Christ's Nativity, it is because the mystery of the Son of God is all embracing. It fills all the time and space of our life. We constantly relive that mystery through the liturgical celebration of the Church, where it is re-actualized and made accessible to us. The daily cycle of services, which prepares for and culminates in the Holy Eucharist, sanctifies time itself, and thereby it sanctifies every moment of our daily existence. Because we are bound by chronology, we can only celebrate the mystery of Christ's saving presence diachronically: in discreet moments, from day to day, from feast to feast. Yet in each of those moments the entire mystery is present to us, from Christ's incarnation to His resurrection and glorification, together with our life-giving incorporation in Him. To celebrate one Feast, therefore, is to celebrate them all. There is no separation, no hiatus, between Annunciation and Nativity, or between Nativity and Pascha. At every feast (and every day is festal) we celebrate, remember and thus relive the one great and awesome Mystery of God's eternal love and our eternal salvation.

Throughout the entire liturgical year we celebrate the inestimable gift—the priceless "treasure in the field"—of that mystery. We do so for ourselves, and we do so for those around us, Christians and others, who find themselves adrift in a sea of moral confusion and radical unbelief.

With the angel Gabriel, we herald the glad tidings, the Annunciation of joy, that the eternal Word of God has—in fact, in all reality—become the Son of the Virgin, that in Him God has truly visited His people to grant them life. And with the Mother of God, together with the heavenly host and the saints of every age, we rejoice. We rejoice and we celebrate, for *today* the eternal mystery is revealed. *Today* we are given to know that God in His infinite otherness is nevertheless here, present with us.

4
Lenten Asceticism

*I*N A REMARKABLE LITTLE BOOK entitled *Body of Death and of Glory*, the French Orthodox theologian and historian, Olivier Clément speaks of the fundamental reason for Christian asceticism:

Asceticism can only be understood in the perspective of the resurrected, liturgical body. Asceticism signifies the effort to strip away our masks, those neurotic identities that usurp our personal vocation. It is an effort based not on will power, but on a ceaseless abandonment of oneself to grace. . . . Asceticism is the struggle, the self-abandonment of openness and faith, which allows the Spirit to transform the anonymous body of our species into a body of 'language' that expresses both the person and communion among persons. Thanks to this ascetic struggle, we are gradually transformed from an acquisitive body, that treats the world as its prey, into a *body of celebration*, that unites itself to the ecclesial liturgy and thereby to the cosmic liturgy.[2]

The aim of the Church's ascetic practices is nothing other than to effect this change, to bring about a radical transformation of the person, from a body of death to a glorified body, a body of celebration.

---

[2]*Corps de mort et de gloire. Petite introduction à une théopoétique du corps* (Paris: Desclée de Brouwer, 1995), 49. Emphasis added.

Caught up in a raging battle between his desire for God and the "law of sin" that holds him captive, the apostle Paul cries out, "Wretched man that I am! Who will deliver me from this body of death?" (Rom 7:24) He answers the question with a doxology: "Thanks be to God through Jesus Christ our Lord!"

God has prepared us, created and blessed us, "for glory" (Rom 9:23). "You have died," Paul tells the Colossians, "and your life is hid with Christ in God. When Christ appears—He who is your life—then you also will appear with Him in glory!" (Col 3:3–4). Caught up in a world of sin, dwelling in a "body of sin" subject to death and corruption, we are nevertheless called, "destined," to participate fully in the glory of the Risen Christ. Through ascetic practice, as through eucharistic communion, that participation becomes a present reality that little by little transforms our body of death into a true body of life and celebration.

This is the perspective that makes sense out of our lenten asceticism. Against this perspective there is the subtle and powerful temptation to turn the Great Fast into an end in itself. We adopt lenten practices of bodily prostrations because of their physical benefit; we abstain from meat and perhaps dairy products in order to purge the body of toxins, or to lose weight, or to be able to say "we did it."

This popular distortion of the reason for lenten discipline goes hand in hand with an obsessive need to "do it right," exemplified by a close examination of every carton we purchase in the grocery store, to be sure it contains not a trace of meat or dairy. We pride ourselves on our ability to sacrifice some pleasure (movies, alcohol, sex, ice cream), at least during the first and fifth weeks of Great Lent. Yet the Old Adam remains very much alive. Our sacrifice all too often translates into narcissistic self-congratulation and all too seldom issues in self-giving love. We still harbor the same old grudges, still neglect the anonymous undesirables in our neighborhoods, and still take vengeance when the opportunity arises. In St Basil's words, we abstain from meat yet devour our brother!

The true aim of all ascetic practice is to allow grace to work within us. It is to allow the Holy Spirit to transform our acquisitive self, our body of death, into a body of celebration. As Clément points out, that transformation requires that we unite ourselves to the "ecclesial liturgy," the ongoing worship of the Church. And this in turn unites us with the "cosmic liturgy," the ceaseless worship of all those who have passed into eternal life.

If we abstain from certain foods, increase and deepen our personal and corporate prayer, devote more time and attention to Scripture and the writings of the Holy Fathers, and intentionally share with others the riches with which God has blessed us, it is for one fundamental purpose: to allow the Holy Spirit to work within us the transformation from a body of death to a body of glory.

Furthermore, and most importantly, these lenten practices, that we glibly and pridefully refer to as "sacrifices," can gradually become every day actions that mark and restructure our entire life.

Lenten asceticism, in other words, is not something exceptional that we assume because of tradition ("we always did it that way") or because of obligation (we feel guilty if we don't). Lenten asceticism is an invitation, a call to something greater, more beautiful and more fulfilling than anything our ordinary experience can offer. Beginning with a call to repentance, to a genuine and deep-seated cleansing and renewal of our very being, it leads gradually to heights of illumination, a vision of the glory to come. Lenten asceticism is an appeal, addressed to us by God Himself, to recognize and to acknowledge that He alone is the object of every true desire, every authentic longing we can know.

Insofar as we heed this appeal, we discover that each day of our life can be viewed and lived in the joyful sorrow of the Lenten spring. We find, to our astonishment and our delight, that every gesture and every attitude can be shaped by an eager anticipation that there will be fulfilled for us the humbling yet sublime promise uttered by the apostle Paul: that our own lowly

body will, in the end, be transformed into the glorious Body of
Jesus Christ (Phil 3:21).

5
Palamas Sunday

ITURGY IS, IN ESSENCE, WORSHIP: praise and glorification of the Holy Trinity. It also serves to glorify the saints and to convey to us the significance of their lives within the Church of their time and ours. This includes important aspects of their teaching. Liturgical services dedicated to the saints provide us with theological understanding, just as they offer us models of moral rectitude and pious conduct.

One such cycle of services is served on the second Sunday of Great Lent and dedicated to the life and work of St Gregory Palamas (1296–1359), sometime Archbishop of Thessalonica and one of the most important of the Byzantine theologians. His most familiar and significant work is the *Triads in Defense of the Holy Hesychasts*, a defense of Athonite monks who claimed to have direct experience of God, including visions of the Uncreated Light.

With the exception of the matins canons, the services of this Sunday were composed by Patriarch Philotheos Coccinus of Constantinople in 1368, the year of Gregory's canonization. They focus particularly on Gregory's triumph over the Calabrian theologian Barlaam, who denied that direct knowledge of God is possible and held that the experience of the Athonite monks was mere delusion.

These services, however, including the second canon dedicated specifically to Gregory, are largely limited to terms of praise that exalt the person of the saint rather than his teaching. They are replete with language such as we find in the verses of "Lord I Call" (Vespers). There Gregory is described as "the trumpet of theology," "the river of wisdom and candlestick of the light," "the well-tuned harp of the Spirit," and "the glory of Thessalonica." They say practically nothing of Gregory's teachings. Only in the *Ikos* of matins do we find allusions to his insights concerning the Divine Light, a distinction between God's "essence" and "energy," together with mention of St Gregory's victory over heresy.

These exalted expressions of praise certainly have their place in our worship. Yet they can only leave us with a desire for more. Just after the final Pascha he celebrated with us here on earth, I asked Fr John Meyendorff—the most outstanding of contemporary Palamas scholars—if he would attempt to compose further services to the saint which would bring out the significance of his theology for the life and faith of Orthodox people. He replied that such a project required someone who was both a poet and a specialist in liturgy. Since I am neither, until now the idea has rested quietly on an upper shelf.

Unlike the fixed canon of Scripture, liturgical services can and should expand whenever inspiration and creativity combine to offer the Church new expressions of its belief and worship.

If some gifted person felt called to elaborate on the existing tradition for Palamas Sunday, perhaps he or she could include, among many others, the following elements of Gregory's teaching.

Palamas is particularly associated with the "hesychast" tradition of mental prayer that is a natural expression of the human mind, popularized in the form of the "Jesus Prayer" or "Prayer of the Heart." More broadly, Palamas taught that through inner, mental prayer—which is a possibility for everyone by virtue of our creation "in the image of God"—the human person can participate directly in the very life of God, through the "divine energies" that are expressions of the divine nature, or essence. Essence and energies are to be understood not as distinct parts of God, but (in Lossky's terms) as "two different modes of the existence of God, within His nature and outside His nature; the same God remains totally inaccessible in His essence—and communicates Himself totally by grace."[3] The aim of hesychast prayer is ultimately *theōsis*, deification of the human person. This signifies that through our experience of God it is possible for us to know God, and to participate in Him both in this life and beyond: here and now through our baptism into Christ, and after death through our resurrection in Him.

Without entering into the finer points of Gregory's dispute with Barlaam, or overwhelming our faithful with technical theological language, the inspired, creative poet we are seeking could easily find material for new services dedicated to this remarkable theologian whom we celebrate on Lent's second Sunday. Another canon, other verses for "Lord I Call" and the aposticha, new troparia: all are possible.

The Liturgy, once again, is a living expression of our faith and our life in Christ. It is appropriate, even necessary, that we strive continually to deepen and enrich its content. Far from violating Holy Tradition, this kind of creative contribution can make the Liturgy alive in the fullest way. And thereby it can serve its most basic purpose: to enrich our life, as it did the life of St Gregory and the Athonite monks, by guiding us along the pathway toward the Uncreated Light.

---

[3]Vladimir Lossky, *The Vision of God* (Crestwood, N.Y.: St Vladimir's Seminary Press, 1983), 157.

6

A Lenten Reading

ORTHODOX CHRISTIANITY CALLS US to live on two different but intimately related levels. One is the level of daily experience: life in family and on the job, paying bills and doing the shopping, cutting the grass and getting the kids to their various activities. It is also life marked by anxiety in a world of war and political upheaval, of poverty, violence and natural disasters. For many people, it is a life that Thomas Hobbes aptly described as "solitary, poor, nasty, brutish and short."

Yet there is another level, another reality that can radically transform our daily routine and even the tenor of the world around us. It is the level of our faith, where celebration of the Paschal mystery turns every Sunday and feast day into the First and Eighth Day of the New Creation, enabling us to participate already here and now in the coming glory of the kingdom of God.

This second level, this other realm or dimension of our life, is one of prayer and silent meditation, of life-giving communion, of joyous celebration, and of healing, reconciling love.

A major reason for the Lenten journey is to equip us for the spiritual warfare necessary to hold these two levels together. As problems and tensions mount in our personal and collective life, we are constantly tempted to focus on one level or the other. Either we give in to the secularizing pressures of the society we live in and pay mere lip service to the faith, power and authority of Orthodox Christianity; or we reject the reality of this world by seeking solace in the esthetically beautiful worship of a comfortable church of our own making. Either of these choices merely deepens the compartmentalization of our life and activity. And we wonder why the experience of Sunday morning seems to have so little to do with the realities and urgencies of Monday.

As we move each year through the Lenten fast—in a world of conflict, brutality and injustice—it is important to remember what Scripture and the rest of the Church's Tradition tell us about this world. Although the fact is hardly reflected in the morning's headlines, the world was created, and is constantly being re-created, by the God of love and mercy, whose deepest desire is to lead everyone, including ourselves, to the perfection and joy of eternal communion in the life of the Holy Trinity. This is a world where people of faith can behold the hand of God in everyday miracles of forgiveness and reconciliation; and in more astounding miracles of unexpected healings, weeping icons, and self-sacrifice.

This is God's world, and we are part of it. As such, our primary calling is to announce and to live out the Paschal message of salvation and eternal life, offered through the victory of Christ over the powers of sin and death.

To do so, however—to facilitate the transformation of the fallen world into a world of faith and love—requires that we devote our time and our energy to the arduous work of inner transformation and spiritual awakening. The Lenten period invites us to do this by increasing our prayer, by fasting, by giving more attention to the poor and needy around us, and by nourishing ourselves with frequent readings from Scripture and the Holy Fathers. I'd like to conclude here with a word about these readings.

Of the many appropriate passages from patristic sources that can provide Lenten nourishment, one of the most powerful and beautiful concludes the Paschal homily by Melito of Sardis, composed toward the end of the second century. Quiet and repeated meditation on its vision of Christ offers one way to unite the two levels, to lift our broken and weary world to the very heights of heaven.

"I am your freedom," Christ declares.
"I am the Passover of salvation,
I am the Lamb slaughtered for you,
I am your ransom,
I am your life,
I am your light,
I am your salvation,
I am your resurrection,
I am your King.
I shall raise you up by my right hand,
I will lead you to the heights of heaven,
There shall I show you the everlasting Father."

He it is who made the heaven and the earth,
And formed humanity in the beginning,
Who was proclaimed through the law and the prophets,
Who took flesh from a virgin,
Who was hung on a tree,
Who was buried in the earth,
Who was raised from the dead,
And ascended to heaven,
Who sits at the right hand of the Father,
Who has the power to save all things,
Through whom the Father acted from the beginning and
    forever.

This is the alpha and omega,
This is the beginning and the end,
The ineffable beginning and the incomprehensible end.
This is the Christ,
This is the King,
This is Jesus,

This is the commander,
This is the Lord,
This is He who rose from the dead,
This is He who sits at the right hand of the Father,
He bears the Father and is borne by him.
To Him be the glory and the might for ever! Amen.[4]

[4]*On Pascha*, Alistair Stewart-Sykes, trans., Popular Patristics Series 20 (Crestwood, N.Y.: St Vladimir's Seminary Press, 2001), 65–67.

7

"Today, a Sacred Pascha"

ORTHODOX THEOLOGY, LIKE HOLY SCRIPTURE, accomplishes what in strictly human terms is not possible. It takes the ineffable and incomprehensible mystery of God's being and activity, and makes it intelligible and accessible.

Most of the images we have of God are pitifully inadequate. Our minds are simply not able to grasp the reality of God, either as Creator or as Redeemer. All the less can they sound the depths of His being. Those depths, as the apostle Paul affirms, can only be fathomed by God Himself in the Person of the Holy Spirit (1 Cor 2:10–11).

The entire universe—and parallel universes, if in fact they exist—results from God's creative activity. This includes the "macrocosmos," the domain of warped space and black holes, as it does the "microcosmos," the realm of unimaginably small elementary particles that constitute material reality. Then there is the immaterial: angels, principalities and powers, together with the human spirit. From galaxy-generating nebulae to the nanosphere, God's creative work, even within the limits of the physical universe, defies understanding. If we affirm His presence in it at all, it is only because Scripture, ecclesial Tradition and the natural order itself reveal that presence to us.

God's work of redemption and salvation are likewise known only by divine revelation. The God who brings all things from nonexistence into being reveals Himself as the God who knows us more intimately than we can ever know ourselves, who loves us to the point that He sacrifices Himself for us, in order to make accessible to us the gift of eternal life. The God beyond the cosmos is also the God who is "closer to us than our own heart."

The mystery of God becomes all the more unfathomable when we consider His inner being. If we know God to be a communion of three Persons, united in a single divine essence or nature, it is only because He has revealed Himself to us as such. Trinitarian theology could never be the product of human logic or human speculation. Yet for those who live "in Christ," the reality of Trinitarian communion becomes self-evident, since we are given the grace to share intimately and personally in that communion ourselves. Every prayer we offer, every worship service we celebrate, every gesture of disinterested love we make confirms what we know of God's innermost reality. His Being is a "being in communion,"[5] and that communion is love. The Father is the source, the *archē* or principle of all life, both human and divine. As such, He eternally brings forth the Son, His Word, by "generation," and the Spirit, His divine Breath or life-giving power, by "procession."

What these terms actually mean remains beyond our comprehension. "What is this proceeding?" St Gregory the Theologian asks. "You explain the ingeneracy of the Father and I will give you a biological account of the Son's begetting and the Spirit's proceeding—and let us go mad, the pair of us, for prying into God's secrets!"[6] If this specific language is given to us, it is because generation and procession speak of certain relationships within the Trinity, both personal and hierarchical. But as St Gregory makes clear, to pry too deeply into the mystery of those relationships is to risk going insane.

St John Chrysostom also spoke (eloquently!) of the "incomprehensibility of God." Therein lies the paradox. The subject of God's being is one that defies not only rational analysis, but even the

---

[5]To recall an expression made popular by Metropolitan John Zizioulas.
[6]*Theological Oration* 31.8.

most elementary attempts at understanding. For this reason, Orthodox theologians adopt an "apophatic" approach to divine mystery, attempting to grasp the incomprehensible and express the ineffable by a *via negativa*: by discerning what God is not, before affirming who and what He is. This, too, is why popular images of God inevitably fail: the Good Lord, the cosmic Santa, "The Force" or what have you. Hence the First and Second Commandments, and the refusal in authentic iconographic tradition to depict the Father in any way at all. The mystery is absolute. It reduces us to silence.

Yet astonishingly, marvelously, that unfathomable mystery is one that any little child can understand, appreciate and, to some degree, convey to others. Those children who can sing from the heart, "Jesus loves me, this I know!" have understood a basic and essential truth of the gospel. We may smile, or be annoyed, at little children who come into church and run up to the analoy to kiss the cross stitched on its covering. Yet they easily convert their focus on the cross into love for Him who bore that cross. If they are guided with gentleness and affection, those children also come quickly to feel whatever anticipation and excitement their parents may experience as Holy Week or other fasting periods lead progressively into a great feast. They may not be able to articulate the complexities of dogma or master the rubrics of liturgical services (although many can recite long portions of those services, particularly the Divine Liturgy). Nevertheless, they are fully capable of grasping and experiencing what is essential.

They know that God loves them from the depths of His heart; that Jesus is their friend and constant companion, always available in times of need; and that the power of God, the Holy Spirit, dwells in them, to guide, bless and protect them as they journey toward Heaven. Their concepts may be simple and naïve. The language they use to explain the basics of the faith may be elementary and embarrassingly anthropomorphic. Yet these children know the truth and speak it, for the simple reason that God has revealed it to them.

The season before and after Holy Pascha, like any other, has always been marked by a great deal of tension and tragedy. Just in the last few months, war, genocide, incurable disease and natural disasters have devastated entire populations. In the face of it all, our theological language can sound obtuse and irrelevant, both to our own needs and to those of the suffering world around us. Yet it is important not to lose sight of our real calling, which is to become like little children.

The Paschal mystery is worthy of our deepest theological reflection, as it is of our most solemn and beautiful liturgical celebration. For us to be worthy of that mystery in return, we need to assume the Church's discipline of fasting, prayer, and readings in our theological and spiritual tradition, together with charitable gestures that bring God's loving presence expressed in theology and liturgy into the realm of day-to-day life. It's a complicated matter, one so demanding that we may find it overwhelming.

It is enough, though, to "become like a little child." We may never quite understand how children seem to fathom the divine mystery, perceive both the tragedy and the glory in Christ's sacrifice, and dwell peacefully and intimately in communion with the Holy Trinity. But they do, and that gives us hope.

In a lost and tormented world, we prepare once again to celebrate a "sacred Pascha." Throughout Holy Week we will journey with our Lord as He makes His way from the suffering of His crucifixion toward the victory and joy of His resurrection. We will hear, sing and celebrate the mystery of our redemption, our liberation from the corrupting powers of sin and death. Finally, we will rejoice at the angel's message spoken in the Empty Tomb: "He is not here, He is risen!"

For that Paschal celebration to be truly sacred requires only that we receive it like a little child, that we stand wide-eyed in breathless anticipation before the mystery of divine Presence and divine Love. *Today* this sacred Pascha is revealed to us. May God grant us the grace to embrace that awesome and beautiful mystery, and the simplicity and openness of heart to be embraced by it.

8

Bright Sadness

THE BEAUTIFUL EXPRESSION, "BRIGHT SADNESS," came back to me with special poignancy during Holy Week this year. In Greek the compound noun is *charmolypē*, variously translated "bitter joy," "joyful mourning," or "affliction that leads to joy." It expresses what the Fathers of the Church call an "antinomy," a truth that defies normal logic. The word is an oxymoron of sorts, which describes a paradoxical spiritual state characterized by a profound mingling of joy and grief. St John of Sinai formulates the idea in the seventh step of his *Ladder of Divine Ascent*, where he speaks of it as "the blessed joy-grief of holy compunction."[7]

In his classic work, *Great Lent*, Fr Alexander Schmemann describes "Sad brightness" as "the sadness of my exile, of the waste I have made of my life; the brightness of God's presence and forgiveness, the joy of the recovered desire for God, the peace of the recovered home."[8] It is sadness that permeates the Lenten season, with its long, fatiguing, magnificent liturgical services and its constant call to repentance. Yet it is a sadness leavened by a deep joy that only tears can adequately express. Tears of longing for the glory and peace to come, for the recovered home where the Father

---

[7]Trans. by Archim. Lazarus Moore (London: Faber & Faber, Ltd.; repr. Willits, Calif.: Eastern Orthodox Books, 1973), 113.

[8](Crestwood, N.Y.: St Vladimir's Seminary Press, 1969), 36.

embraces each of us, His prodigal children, with an unfathomable depth of forgiving love.

That bright sadness puts me in touch with a vital sensitivity that I otherwise rarely experience. This past Lent and Holy Week, it enabled me to see for the first time the faces of people I have known, in some cases for years, yet without really seeing them or knowing them very well at all. It happened especially with members of our parish community, many of whom have lived through degrees of hardship and suffering most of us can barely imagine: new immigrants from Russia, Ukraine or Romania, for example, whose faith remained strong despite constant threats, persecution and material deprivation. Or a young couple who just lost their first child four months into the pregnancy; or a recent convert who is attempting to recover from a divorce and the loss of everything he held dear, including his children.

There are many others in the parish, too, who tend to keep to themselves their personal stress and suffering. Yet their eyes and their body language betray the weight of the burdens they carry. Some are caring at home for elderly parents who are afflicted with dementia or alcoholism. Others are struggling to offer love, support and guidance to disruptive or promiscuous adolescents; or depriving themselves in order to feed and clothe their children after their business collapsed or they fell victim to "downsizing."

Multitudes of different stories, yet with one common theme: they long ago placed their trust and their hope in Christ, the source and end of their most intense longing, and in these past few days they gathered together to celebrate their faith and their hope at the Feast of feasts, Holy Pascha.

What produced a truly bright sadness for me this year was not my feeble attempts at fasting or my less than enthusiastic efforts toward repentance. It wasn't even so much the liturgical celebrations, as splendid and moving as they were, and always are. Instead, it was seeing certain faces for the first time. These were faces I had looked at, or spoken to, or shared coffee hour with any number of times. But they had usually seemed rather at a distance:

interesting, intelligent, amusing, often warm and gracious; but
still people whom I hardly knew.

Somehow, by God's grace, I was able during this past Holy Week
to see in those faces new depths of personal joy and suffering, of
hope and selfless attentiveness to others, as well as of spiritual
struggle and fervent commitment to Christ—depths I can't find in
myself, but that reveal themselves so clearly through the strength
and honest simplicity of the witness these people offer to me and
to others around them.

This implies that the grief-filled joy of the Lenten season is
not merely an individual feeling. It is a profoundly ecclesial
experience, one I can know in its painful yet glorious fullness
only insofar as I share it with other people. Through this experience—perhaps more than through any other, apart from
Eucharistic communion itself—we find ourselves joined, in compunction and longing, with all those who make up the universal
Body of Christ.

Bright sadness may be the most powerful and important experience we can know. It brings to our mind and heart, in the most
direct and personal way, the ultimate purpose of our life and the
object or end of our most passionate desire. It reminds us of who
we are, as beloved children of God, created in His image and
invited to glorify and enjoy Him forever.

That conflicted emotion of bright sadness is a blessed gift, bestowed by the God who loves us with a "love without limit."*[9] It
comes to us through our ascetic struggle during the Lenten season, as it does through the solemn beauty of the Church's liturgical services.

But it can come to us as well when we observe it in the people
around us: people with whom and for whom we pray, people who
in many cases pray for us without our being aware of it. We find
that bright sadness in communion with them, in hearing their

[9]This is an expression widely used among Orthodox Christians in Western
Europe, especially under the influence of Fr Lev Gillet, also known as "a monk of
the Eastern Church." He wrote about *l'amour sans limites* and bore witness to it
throughout his life.

stories, in sharing their hopes, fears and longings. We find it through being attentive to the beauty and truth of their life and their unique presence.

We find it once we find them, possibly for the first time: not merely as parishioners, nor even as friends, but as brothers and sisters, united forever in the Body of Christ. Here and now, we share their pains, their struggles and their delights. That bright sadness, though, tells us that one day we will also share with them, in intimate communion, a glory and joy that know no mourning, no grief, no sorrow nor sighing, but only life everlasting.

9
Ecstatic Wonder

ON THE EVE OF THE SUNDAY of the Holy Myrrhbearing Women, the Matins service recalls Christ's resurrection appearances as they are recounted at the close of St Mark's Gospel. If Biblical scholars are correct, these last verses, Mark 16:9–20, did not originally belong to the Gospel narrative. This series of appearances of the risen Lord was apparently gathered together by the early Church for catechetical purposes and was only subsequently added to the Second Gospel to provide it with what seemed to be a more appropriate conclusion.

This means that the original Gospel, as St Mark composed it, in fact ended with the passage read at the Sunday morning Liturgy (Mk 15:42–16:8). The Myrrhbearing Women, having beheld the empty shroud and heard the angelic testimony, were filled with trembling and astonishment—*tromos kai ekstasis*, more precisely rendered "ecstatic wonder." It was this intense emotional response that led them to flee the tomb and, for a while, to say nothing to anyone, "for they were afraid."

Why would the evangelist have ended his narrative in this surprising, almost scandalous way? Especially since we know that the women finally *did* announce to Peter and the other disciples that they had discovered the tomb to be empty, and that an angel had declared to them that Jesus had risen from the dead? Mark addressed his writing to believers: those who were thoroughly familiar with the entire Gospel story, persons whose very life and faith were grounded in the truth and hope of the Resurrection. Why, then, should he conclude his work with the mysterious image of the tomb, together with the women's reaction, rather than depict, as the other evangelists did, the various appearances of the risen Lord to His disciples?

The only plausible answer is that St Mark wanted to stress above all this reaction—this intense inner response—of the women to the vision of the tomb and the evidence of the burial cloths. These women had followed Jesus faithfully throughout the time of His earthly ministry, caring for His needs, providing food and lodging for Him and His disciples as they made their pilgrimage from Galilee through Judea and into the holy city of Jerusalem. They remained faithful to him throughout his Passion, and they assisted in His burial. Then, as the Sabbath drew near, they had to leave the burial ritual uncompleted and return to their homes. That ritual could only be finished after the Sabbath, early on the following Sunday morning.

Very early on that first day of the week, the women gathered aromatic spices and walked to the tomb. Finding the stone rolled away, they entered with trepidation. There they beheld a young man, an angelic figure, seated where the body of Jesus had been laid, where now there was only an empty shroud. Then, filled with trembling and astonishment, with "ecstatic wonder," they fled from the tomb, struck dumb by the vision that had just been granted to them. For the moment they could say nothing to anyone, "for they were afraid."

This fear experienced by the Myrrhbearing Women was not abject terror, a kind of dread before something threatening and indecipherable. Rather, it was the experience of *awe*, so deep and intense that they became ecstatic, beside themselves, removed from the usual sphere of human experience, and granted the degree of self-transcending wonder that the apostle Paul knew when, in an ecstatic trance, he was "caught up into the third heaven, into Paradise" (2 Cor 12).

Such is the emotion that accompanies the experience of a theophany, a revelation of divine power and majesty. This is the emotion that seized the women in the empty tomb. They beheld the linen shroud and heard the angel's assurance that Jesus, who was dead, had been raised to life. They saw, they were amazed, and they left the tomb in a spirit of wonder and awe-filled silence.

As the memory of the paschal celebration fades in the days and weeks following the feast, we are offered in the Myrrhbearing Women an image—a living icon—of paschal wonder, ecstatic wonder. If we listen attentively to the magnificent hymns of the Pentacostarion,[10] we can hear the angelic announcement they heard and share the wonder that was theirs. In the midst of our ordinariness—shopping, taking the kids to school, fussing with the computer, sitting through office meetings, fighting traffic, or battling anxieties in the middle of the night—in the midst of all of it, that image of the Myrrhbearing Women extends an invitation. It calls us to step out of ourselves for a while, and with them to enter the tomb where Jesus was laid out in death. It calls us to contemplate the ineffable mystery of the empty shroud, together with the angelic proclamation, "He is not here, He is risen!"

Out of that silent contemplation can come once again the profound sense of awe, of ecstatic wonder, that seized the women and all those who beheld the risen Lord. As it did for the apostle Paul, that awe and that wonder can lift us out of our ordinariness, if only for a moment, and give us a glimpse, a blessed foretaste, of Paradise.

[10] The book of Orthodox liturgical services from matins of Pascha (Easter) until the Sunday after Pentecost, the Sunday of All Saints.

10

"Through Your Glorious Ascension"

PSALM 67/68 IS CONSIDERED BY MOST biblical scholars to be the most difficult of all psalms to interpret.[11] The current consensus holds that the psalm was an ancient cultic hymn, originally recited during an autumn festival by the covenant-community of Israel. Its theme celebrates the coming of God to His people, from Sinai to Zion, in order to actualize in their midst His past mighty works of salvation. This actualization then leads the people toward the eschatological future, the age to come, when God's glory and majesty will be recognized and acknowledged by all the nations of the earth.

As difficult to interpret as many may find it to be, this psalm, with its opening cry, "Let God arise!" is nevertheless one of the most familiar biblical pronouncements of the Orthodox paschal season. It begins with what the Church recognizes as a prophetic announcement of our Lord's resurrection. This is complemented by what biblical and patristic tradition sees as allusions to Christ's ascension and the sending of the Holy Spirit at Pentecost. St Paul offers this interpretation in his letter to the Ephesians, where he modifies, in a minor yet significant way, the Septuagint version of Psalm 67: "When He ascended on high, He led a host of captives,

---

[11]For example, A. Weiser, *The Psalms* (Philadelphia: Westminster, 1962), 481; see also the *Oxford Annotated Bible (RSV)*, (New York: Oxford, 1965), 704 note, repeated in the *Oxford NRSV* (New York: Oxford, 1991), 728 note.

and He gave gifts to men" (Eph 4:8). Those gifts, as the apostle declares, include the *charismata*, the "spiritual gifts" or gift of the Spirit Himself, bestowed upon the Church for the preaching of the gospel and the upbuilding of the Body of Christ.

Another theme appears throughout this letter, also derived from Psalm 67/68. By his descent into the "depths of the earth," into the heart of the fallen creation, Christ destroys the power of sin and death. And by His ascension in glory, He "fills all things with Himself" (Eph 4:9–10). This is the same message proclaimed by the Gospel of John: "No one has ascended into heaven but He who descended from heaven, the Son of Man," and this, to work out salvation and eternal life for all those who believe (Jn 3:13–15).

The entire Christian mystery is expressed by this double movement of descent and ascension, the incarnation and glorification of the eternal Son of God. As Orthodox spiritual and liturgical tradition affirms, this movement was undertaken not for Christ's own sake, but for ours. Through His incarnation, the Son of God took upon Himself our very life and being, the specific conditions of our human nature, in order to restore that nature to its original perfection, and to open the way for us to ascend with Him to the heights of heaven, there to share with Him His own glory and majesty.

Elaborating on this theme, St Irenaeus of Lyon declares in his treatise *Against Heresies* (III.19.3):

> The Lord himself gave us a sign . . . A virgin conceived and bore a son, 'God with us' (Is 7:14). He descended into the depths of the earth to seek the lost sheep, His own handiwork, which He Himself had made. Then He ascended into the heights above, to offer and submit to His Father this humanity (*hominem*) which had been found, becoming Himself the firstfruits of man's resurrection.

A familiar prayer, attributed to St Symeon Metaphrastes (a midtenth century Byzantine hagiographer) and included in the Orthodox prayers before communion, recounts the unfolding of events

in Christ's life, death and glorification, together with their spiritual
and moral significance for believers:

> Through *Your life-giving resurrection* You raised up the first father
> who had fallen. Raise me up, for I am sunk in sin, and give me the
> image of repentance.

> Through *Your glorious ascension* You made the flesh that You
> assumed to be divine and placed it on the throne at the Father's
> right hand. Grant me to receive a place at the right hand with the
> saved through communion of Your Holy Mysteries.

By His incarnation, Christ deified the flesh, the body with its
human nature, and thus He restored it to the perfection and glory
for which God originally intended it. As the First Adam, the arche-
type of all human existence, and as the Last Adam, the Author of
Life who gives life to those who dwell in Him, Christ ascends in
his divine flesh, exalting newly perfected human nature with Himself. The throne is the image that symbolizes that exaltation. By
placing His deified flesh on the throne at the "right hand of the
Father," God the Son makes the ultimate sacramental gesture,
offering our own fallen yet restored nature to Him who is the
Source of all life, both human and divine. Because of our incorporation into the life of the Son, we can hope to join with the saints,
the host of the saved. Yet this hope is already partially realized,
insofar as we partake of that divine life here and now by participating in the Holy Eucharist.

A further refinement of this theme is offered to us by the great
Byzantine mystic, St Gregory of Sinai (†1346). In the chapter from
the *Philokalia* known as "Further Texts,"[12] St Gregory describes in
eloquent terms the correspondence between the descending,
ascending movement of Christ and spiritual growth in our own
life. The passage is worth quoting in full:

[12]*Alia Capita*; PG 150.1300.

Everyone baptized into Christ should pass progressively through all the stages of Christ's own life, for in baptism he receives the power so to progress, and through the commandments he can discover and learn how to accomplish such progression. To Christ's conception corresponds the foretaste of the gift of the Holy Spirit, to His nativity the actual experience of joyousness, to His baptism the cleansing force of the fire of the Spirit, to His transfiguration the contemplation of divine light, to His crucifixion the dying to all things, to His burial the indwelling of divine love in the heart, to His resurrection the soul's life-quickening resurrection, and to His ascension divine ecstasy and the transport of the intellect into God.[13]

To most of our contemporaries, this kind of interpretation of the events in Christ's life seems odd if not scandalous. It strikes them as pure allegorizing: taking the historical events of Christ's passion, death and resurrection, and reading them as metaphors to describe our inner spiritual state, the condition of the human soul.

To those of us who, in the days following Holy Pascha, have sung out, "Let God arise!" and have tasted the heavenly gifts of his glorified Body and Blood, who have embraced others and been embraced with reconciling love "even by those who hate us," this correspondence between the events of Christ's life and our own is self-evident. Yesterday we were crucified with Him; today we rise with Him in glory. Yesterday He descended into the lower parts of the earth, into the darkness of our own being and experience; today we ascend with Him in newness of life, in a potentially deified flesh, in order to take our place with Him at the right hand of God the Father.

By His glorious ascension, Christ has already spoken to our deepest longing and fulfilled our most fervent hope. He has taken us as He took the hand of Adam, depicted in the Paschal icon of

---

[13]"Further Texts" 1, in *The Philokalia*, vol. 4, ed. by G.E.H. Palmer, Ph. Sherrard and K. Ware (London: Faber & Faber, 1995), 253.

the descent into Hades. He has raised us up with Himself, out of the grave of our own making, and ascended with us into the awesome and blessed presence of His Father. He has transported into the very presence of God our "intellect," our spiritual perception of transcendent life and being. And in so doing, He has led us— even in the mundane affairs of our daily existence—into the joyful and healing state of divine ecstasy.

11
"By Your Holy Spirit"

I N HIS "REFLECTIONS ON THE KNOWLEDGE OF GOD," Saint Silouan of Mount Athos (†1938) speaks in a very simple and beautiful way of the presence and power of the Holy Spirit in the lives of the faithful.[14] They are words that seem especially significant in the time of Pentecost, when we celebrate and relive the coming of the Spirit in power, to renew us and all of creation.

The Spirit, Silouan declares, brought him through torments of doubt to the firm conviction that "Jesus Christ is God." This Spirit, who bestows the gift of faith, fills every aspect of our life and leads us progressively towards the twin goals of Knowledge of God and Love of Enemies. This is no ordinary knowledge, as he declares; nor is that love the result of human effort, of bending our will and feelings until we no longer react with fear and hostility toward those who threaten us. Knowledge and love, rather, are closely linked gifts of divine grace. If we can know anything at all of God, and even enter into the most intimate communion with Him, it is only because God grants us this mystical knowledge by His Spirit, who dwells within the temple of the heart. If we can love even our enemy, it is only with the

---

[14]Archim. Sophrony, *St Silouan the Athonite* (Crestwood, N.Y.: St Vladimir's Seminary Press, 1999), 353ff.

compassion and mercy of God Himself, who infuses our heart with the transforming grace of the Spirit. This is a grace that lifts us above our passions—corrupted feelings of victimization and shame, of anxiety and defensive rage—and enables us, in the power of the Spirit, to embrace with love even those who hate us, who threaten us, and who, on a purely human level, inspire our contempt and loathing.

But just who is this enemy? We live in an age that inspires a certain paranoia, and with it an all too easy identification of those who deserve this label. After 9/11, it is tempting to think of the enemy as the incarnation of evil, a person or group that threatens our way of life or even life itself. From Hitler, Stalin and Pol Pot, we have moved on to Saddam Hussein, Osama bin Laden and jihadists in general. We have become (understandably) so obsessed with the enemy "out there" that we tend to overlook the truth famously uttered by Walt Kelly through his cartoon character Pogo: "We have met the enemy and he is us."

One of the greatest and most illuminating gifts we receive from the Spirit is recognition and acceptance of the fact that we are often our own worst enemy. It is that burdensome fact that can lead us to make enemies even of those who are closest to us, people whom we know intimately and love dearly. Passions of jealousy, fear or frustration can easily turn us against a spouse, a child or a parent. Little irritations can transform an insignificant incident into a household drama that creates tension, alienation and rejection. The child doesn't have to steal or do drugs to bring down our wrath. Coming home after curfew or leaving his room in a mess is often enough to provoke anger and demeaning criticism. A spouse doesn't have to commit adultery or empty the bank account to attain the status of "enemy." It's often enough that she make fun of us in the company of our friends, or lose the car keys, or criticize us for some mistake or failure we committed out of carelessness.

The ascetic life is made up of struggles against just these kinds of temptations, which turn loved ones into candidates for our revenge, or siblings in Christ into outright enemies. These inner struggles are as necessary in monastic life as they are in the home, at the office or on the work site. Wherever people live, work and play in close proximity to one another, where the opportunity exists to share, to serve and to love another person to our mutual benefit and mutual salvation, there exists, too, the possibility to corrupt that relationship. Then affection easily turns to loathing and respect to ridicule. The old song title, "You always hurt the one you love," has become hackneyed, but it expresses an enduring truth.

Whether the enemy is distant or close—the anonymous face of a suicide bomber or the destructive kid who lives next door or upstairs—the passions we experience in their regard cannot be overcome by will power or reason. There needs to be a change of heart that only God can accomplish. "The Lord's love," Silouan declares, "is made known in no other wise than through the Holy Spirit." Through that Spirit we receive knowledge of God and His compassionate mercy, and at the same time we acquire knowledge of and about ourselves. The Spirit holds up before our eyes a mirror, one that reveals the often-unpleasant truth about us. This includes the sad truth of our own failings and our constant temptation to identify the other, rather than ourself, as the ultimate enemy. Yet that mirror also has the capacity to reveal within us the divine image in which we were created, and into which the Spirit constantly re-creates us. And that ongoing work of re-creation, accomplished precisely by the indwelling Holy Spirit, enables us in turn to behold beauty and goodness in the face of others, and particularly of our closest friends and loved ones who have become the objects of our hostility.

The Pentecostal season could be for each of us, as it should be, a time of re-creation and renewal. It could lead to an illumining of the heart and mind that enables us to see ourselves as we truly are, and to love our enemy as he or she truly is, created in the image of God, renewed by the grace and power of the Holy Spirit, and called to eternal communion with the Lord of love.

St Silouan, once again, indicates how we might attain this elusive yet precious goal:

> The man who cries out against evil men but does not pray for them will never know the grace of God.
>
> If you would know of the Lord's love for us, hate sin and evil thoughts, and day and night pray fervently. The Lord will then give you His grace, and you will know Him through the Holy Spirit, and after death, when you enter into paradise, there too, you will know the Lord through the Holy Spirit, as you knew Him on earth.[15]

---

[15]*St Silouan the Athonite*, 357.

12

Prayer in the Spirit

A S WE SETTLE BACK INTO THE "ordinary time" of our liturgical year, it's important to recall the special value and significance of this season. "Ordinary" should be understood as a technical term, which refers to a specific period in our yearly celebration. In the conventional sense, there is nothing ordinary about it at all. From feasts dedicated to saints (the apostles Peter and Paul, St John Baptist, Father Herman of Alaska . . .) to the Great Feasts of Transfiguration and Dormition, this period that concludes the yearly cycle of services is one of exceptional richness.

It is also the period after Pentecost, during which we experience with particular intensity the personal presence and illuminating grace of the Holy Spirit. This experience becomes ours especially in times of prayer, both personal and liturgical.

St Basil the Great develops this theme in a remarkable section of his treatise *On the Holy Spirit*. Chapter 26 discusses the proper usage of the little preposition *in* when we speak of the Spirit and His operations. The Spirit, he says, dwells *in* those who strive to live the life in Christ in the same way that form is present *in* matter. This language goes back to Aristotle, for whom the essence, substance or "form" of a reality exists within that reality itself, rather than on a transcendent ideal plane, as his teacher Plato taught. St Basil uses an Aristotelian understanding of the relation between form and matter to describe the indwelling presence of the Spirit within the saints. Just as the form or essence of a thing exists in and is inseparable from the thing itself, so the Holy Spirit exists and dwells in those who receive Him, and He does so to such an extent and with such transforming power, that "such a person no longer lives according to the flesh, but is led by the Spirit of God. He is called a son of God, because he is conformed to the image of the Son of God; we call him a spiritual man."[16]

This is an extraordinary statement. It means that the Holy Spirit, received initially through baptism and chrismation, actually transforms our very being, our "essence" or "form," to the point that we are "conformed to the image" of Christ. We become "spiritual beings," oriented and directed no longer according to the flesh, but according to the Spirit, who is God Himself.

At the close of this same chapter, St Basil alludes to a passage from the apostle Paul: "The Spirit helps us in our weakness; for we do not know how to pray as we ought, but the Spirit Himself intercedes for us with sighs too deep for words" (Rom 8:26). Basil concludes, "If you remain outside the Spirit, you cannot worship at all, and if you are in Him you cannot separate Him from God. Light cannot be separated from what it makes visible, and it is impossible for you to recognize Christ, the Image of the invisible God, unless the Spirit enlightens you."[17]

This means first of all that authentic worship is possible only through the indwelling power of the Holy Spirit. Yet beyond that, it implies that true prayer is not a human endeavor at all. It is the work of God within us. In prayer, God speaks to God; the Spirit addresses the Father within the temple of the heart. Through that divine work, the Spirit illumines for us and within us the "Face," the image and glory, of the Son. Bathed in the radiant light of that divine Image, we recognize Christ for who He is: we behold Him as Lord and Savior, the Crucified and Risen One. And that Image in turn reveals to us the Face of the Father.

---

[16]St Basil, *On the Holy Spirit* (Crestwood, N.Y.: St Vladimir's Seminary Press, 1980), 93.

[17]Ibid., 97.

Prayer, then, is a constant inner movement of the heart: *in* the Spirit, *through* the Son, *to* the Father. Realized "in spirit and truth" (Jn 4:23)—that is, in the Holy Spirit and in Christ who is the Truth—authentic prayer is a pure gift, bestowed by the Holy Trinity, to illumine and transform our life so thoroughly that it "conforms us to the image of the Son of God."

There is little doubt that for most of us this exalted image of prayer lies far from our daily experience. Throughout the day we may have an ongoing conversation of sorts with God, easily interrupted by the telephone, or a child who needs our attention, or random yet demonic thoughts that intrude on our efforts to pray. We may take a few minutes during the morning or evening to step back and find a little peace and quiet, to read a few lines of Scripture or to offer a few words of intercession for someone we love. But we rarely, if ever, experience being "filled with the Spirit," in the same way that Christians of other confessions often feel themselves to be.

For Orthodox Christians, the experience of the Spirit and of genuine worship usually takes a different form. Remaining wary of the emotional exuberance that can turn worship into a pep rally or reduce it to some sort of spiritual entertainment, we find ourselves truly and deeply moved by the Holy Spirit in the silence of personal meditation, in the solemn beauty of liturgical chant, or through sharing with someone else a prayer of petition or thanksgiving.

We may not pray in tongues, or prophesy, or perform astonishing miracles. But insofar as we remain open to the inner working of the Spirit, allowing Him to intercede for us "with sighs too deep for words," we can be sure that our prayer is real and genuine, that it is heard and welcomed by God. Then in rare moments, by the illumination of that same Spirit, we can actually behold Christ, the Image, and through that illumination find ourselves led into an intense and joy-filled communion with the Father.

13

Eschew Obfuscation

WHEN WE TALK OUR USUAL ORTHODOX "church language," many people haven't the vaguest idea what we're talking about. This was brought home to me in a rather harsh way not long ago, when a lapsed Catholic monk visited our parish. He had heard reports of the beauty of Orthodox worship and the depths of Orthodox spiritual life, and he came to experience some of it for himself.

After he left the monastery and in effect left the Catholic Church, he began working with the disenfranchised: homeless people in particular, including some who had fallen on hard times after years of working in high profile dot-com jobs. Some were uneducated, but most had completed high school, and several held advanced degrees. He served them in a soup kitchen, but his real work consisted in preaching and pastoral counseling, attempting to bring the gospel to them and vice versa.

The Sunday morning Liturgy over, he and I left the church and stopped for a while at coffee hour. When I asked how he felt about his first experience in an Orthodox parish, he scowled and shook his head.

"That's nothing my people could ever relate to," he said. Then he proceeded, in rather unkind terms, to criticize everything from the sermon ("too moralistic") to the repetitious litanies ("Again and again in peace . . . "). His main complaint, however, was leveled against the vocabulary: "churchy jargon," as he called it.

I felt offended and saddened, because I had hoped for a very different reaction. The sermon, delivered by a young and earnest priest who was substituting for the parish rector, was indeed stiff and a little moralizing. But beneath the awkwardness was a solid message that conveyed the gospel to those with ears to hear. The language of the Liturgy itself was sublime, as it has been for centuries. What really was there to complain about?

His argument was essentially that the Liturgy, from vestments to gestures to language, represents something wholly foreign to those who are not raised in Orthodoxy, and particularly those whose parishes and pastors had brought them up with an anti-Catholic and anti-liturgical bias.

When he focused on language as such, he referred to the common expressions we use, not only in liturgy, but also in books and articles whose intention is to impart something of the richness of Orthodox life and faith. The average people on the street, long alienated from any particular religious expression, he insisted, can't begin to wrap their minds around terms such as "eschatology," "redemption," "glorification," "deification," or even "sin." To them the Bible is little more than a collection of stories for kids: Adam and Eve, the Flood, people walking on water, and the like.

"If you Orthodox don't learn to speak to people in the world around you," he concluded, "you'll stay a ghetto church, no matter how much you reorganize yourselves. You may attract a few converts who are looking for some esoteric brand of Christianity, but eventually you'll disappear."

He said all this in such a matter-of-fact way that it was hard to reply. And to my shame, I didn't really try. It did make me think harder than I had before, though, about the way we have developed our own language and what that means for proclaiming Orthodox Christianity to everyone from "cradle" members of our parishes to catechumens and those we call "seekers."

A great deal has already been done to recast traditional language and forms of thought into expressions that convey the essence of the faith to the inquiring non-Orthodox. *Again* magazine and many other publications of Conciliar Press, for example, together with materials from our respective Christian education and youth departments, have gone far to close the language gap between ourselves and the "outside world" of children and young people. And more is being done every day to speak to adults, both in our parishes and elsewhere, in a way that makes the gospel accessible and conveys it with power.

My point here is simply that we Orthodox, as part of our vocational responsibility in this land, need to continue and intensify these efforts. It's very easy for us to forget that we do in fact speak a particular language that in many ways is foreign to those around us, including non-Orthodox members of our families and close friends of other faith traditions. We should not change that language, at least not in any way that alters its meaning. But that meaning needs to be made clear and comprehensible: in liturgical translations, in church school and other catechetical materials, in sermons, and in publications addressed to the general public as evangelistic and apologetic tools.

The urgency for such labor was brought home to me a few days ago by another acquaintance, this time a person who teaches math at the college level. Somehow or other we got onto the subject of mathematical conundrums. The most elusive these days seems to be the "Riemann Hypothesis." He quoted it, and I understood why: "All non-trivial zeros of the zeta function have real part one-half."

Since I nearly flunked first year algebra and can't tell a sine from a surd, his language was as incomprehensible to me as talk of "theosis" and "sacramental grace" is to my Catholic friend's street people.

"Eschew obfuscation." When it comes to proclaiming the gospel, that ironic little admonition couldn't be clearer or more to the point. It's a goal we need to aim for, however hard it may be to attain. Because if the Son of God came as "the Word," He did so to reveal and to enlighten: to make the Truth known, understandable and accessible to us all.

14

The Icon as Mirror

THE FRESCOED HEAD IS ALL THAT remains of an anonymous Ascetic, whose image was reproduced on a card a Catholic friend once gave me, to help guide me on my way toward Orthodoxy.

The reproduction includes a portion of the wall on which, I suppose, this saintly man's entire body once appeared. It's easy to imagine that wall as part of an ancient monastic church, where faithful monks prayed and sang their love for God, before some hostile outside forces sacked the place and left intact only this austere yet strikingly beautiful face. The eyes stare beyond the observer into the abyss of eternity. They are sad eyes, which reflect the suffering of those who lived and died in that place, yet they are also filled with wisdom and a deep calm. They are the eyes of a genuine ascetic, whose gaze also penetrates into the recesses of one's soul.

This sacred image illustrates better than most do, the truth that an authentic icon is more than a window that reveals the beauty of heaven within the limits of time and space. The icon is also a mirror. In it, we behold the face of Christ, His holy Mother and the saints. Yet there we also behold our own true face, the glorified *persona* whom we were created to become. Jesus Christ is the visible image of the invisible God (Col 1; Heb 1). He is also the visible image of ourselves, as we shall be when—one day by the sheer grace of God—we are transformed "from glory to glory" (2 Cor 3) into His own divine likeness.

In the meantime, icons serve to remind us of that sublime calling, that majestic possibility. Yet they also remind us of all that is lacking in our life, all that hinders our progress toward undying communion with the God who loves us. As mirrors, icons speak both promise and judgment.

I experienced this twofold revelation very acutely the first time I visited a saintly old Russian woman in Paris, sometime in the late 1960s. She had fled her native land during the Bolshevik revolution, and after a tortuous journey of several years duration, she ended up as an exile in a small apartment in the Bois de Boulogne, on the outskirts of the city. An icon of John the Forerunner, hanging in a corner of her dusty, book-filled study, brought home to me just how much these holy images indeed do serve both to promise and to judge. That evening, I tried to catch a little of that experience in a simple bit of verse, titled "Baba's Room."

> In a dust-filled corner
> Of her cluttered, musty room
> An ancient icon hangs
> Half hidden by a greasy veil
> Of lampblack—the sacred soot
> Of fervent veneration
> That obscures the very image
> The lampada would reveal.
>
> Dancing lightly on the oil
> The flick'ring flame illumes
> A face unearthly, wreathed
> In an aureole of gold.
> Gazing from the depths
> Of the hollowed wooden frame
> The Baptist's bright sad eyes
> Focus on eternity.

In the stillness, gently broken
By her shuffle through the house,
My inner gaze is drawn, compelled
By those splendid tragic eyes
To fix upon eternity within
Where a once brighter image
Lies yet more obscured, concealed
Behind a darker veil of sin.

Marked by long ascetic toil, that face
Describes with silent eloquence
The painful, blessed way to purity
Of heart. . . . The wild man of the desert
Is a staretz in disguise
Whose eyes perceive and quietly condemn
Mon âme de boue that happily confines
God's image in obscurity.

The eyes of this anonymous Ascetic, like those of the Baptist, peer deep into the dark places of my soul. They perceive what I can barely admit to myself or even to my father-confessor: spiritual sins of pride, doubt, faithlessness and fear—all manner of foolish and hurtful things done "with knowledge or in ignorance," together with endless other things left undone: gestures of charity and friendship, words of reconciliation and compassion.

Yet those eyes also direct my own gaze beyond the superficial, mundane affairs of every day, and enable me, like them, to focus on eternity.

Icons open a window, to reveal the beauty of heaven. At the same time, they mirror the divine image in which each of us was created. And thereby—despite our insufficiencies and occasional ugliness—they reveal the beauty that is in us as well.

15
Divine Symmetry

BEAUTY IS OFTEN EXPRESSED BY symmetry or balanced proportions. Musical compositions and graphic art usually strive for some measure of symmetry, in order to appeal to our esthetic tastes. They provide us with a sense of harmony, stability and peace—even a sense of sanity, within an often chaotic and crazy world. Major theological themes do the same.

The New Testament depicts Christ's saving work by stressing its symmetrical movement. "No one has ascended into heaven," Jesus declares," but He who descended from heaven, the Son of Man" (John 3:13). The apostle Paul elaborates on this imagery in the sublime christological hymn of Philippians 2:5–11. He who from all eternity is "equal" with God the Father, who bears the divine "form" or essence of God, descends through His incarnation to take upon Himself the "form" of a man, the essence or nature of created humanity. Because of His humble obedience, sealed by His death on the Cross, the Father "highly exalts" Him, and reveals Him, in the presence of all of creation, to be "Kyrios," both Lord and God.

A similar symmetry characterizes the whole of salvation history. Creation and the people of Israel are balanced and fulfilled by a new creation of the "Israel of God," the Church (Gal 6:16). And the pivot or fulcrum that achieves and maintains that balance is the coming in the flesh of the Son of God.

We find this kind of symmetry as well in iconography, perhaps nowhere more strikingly than in certain images of Christ and His holy Mother. The iconostasis or icon screen of any Orthodox church invariably includes, on the left side of the Royal Doors as viewed by the worshiper, an image of Mary, the Mother of God, holding her divine Son. In the most typical images, He is enthroned upon her, as she offers Him to the faithful and to the world. She embraces her Son with tender affection. Yet at the same time her *regard* is directed outward, toward the congregation and toward eternity. This child she has borne will suffer and die, in order to open the way that leads both her and us to life in the kingdom of heaven.

Here there is a symmetry, an exquisite balance, between Mother and Child, between joy and sadness, between holding and relinquishing, as there is between new life that has emerged from the womb and the impending death that will make possible a new order of Life beyond.

Yet this image fits into a greater symmetry, insofar as it is fulfilled by the movement represented in the icon of the Dormition or "Falling Asleep of the Mother of God." This icon depicts the apostles, who "from all the ends of the earth have gathered in Gethsemane." They surround the Theotokos, the Mother of God, as she lies "asleep" in a position reminiscent of Jesus' own repose, His lifeless body outstretched in the new tomb. In some images, St John—the Beloved Disciple, into whose hands Christ committed His Mother—bends over her as she bent over her deceased Son. In others, St John is shown at the foot of the bier, his hands pointing toward the Virgin in a gesture of profound veneration. In the center, behind the bier, stands the glorified Christ. A fourteenth-century Novgorod icon shows Him vested in gold, with a flaming seraph above and behind His head. In His arms He holds a small figure that represents His mother's soul, dressed in radiant white. That garment, however, is a burial shroud, recalling the winding sheet that enfolded her Son at His own burial.

That winding sheet was first seen at Christ's Nativity, when the newborn child was wrapped, not in the garb of an infant, but in the shroud of a dead man. Now, at her Dormition, Mary's soul appears vested in a similar shroud, yet one transfigured by light. The Risen Lord embraces His holy Mother as she embraced Him at His birth. As she offered Him to the worshipers and to the world, so He now, in similar fashion, offers her. And as she surrendered Him to life-giving death, so He receives her from death, to raise her with Himself to eternal life.

There is symmetry—balanced proportion—throughout it all, from image to image and within each individual depiction. It is a divine symmetry that produces beauty, peace and harmony, both in the icon itself and in those who pray before it.

This symmetry tells the story of our own experience, from birth through death, and on to life beyond. For what began with Christ and His holy Mother comes to completion with us, as He raises us from our own death and unites us with her in the glory of the communion of saints.

IV

Our Life in Christ

1

"Why?"

OVER A YEAR HAS PASSED SINCE the devastating tsunami in the Indian Ocean took hundreds of thousands of lives and left millions homeless and destitute. During the weeks following that horrendous event, mudslides, blizzards, floods and other natural disasters exacted their toll as well, in California and throughout the world. Most recently, Hurricane Katrina leveled and flooded the Gulf Coast, leaving hundreds of people dead and hundreds of thousands more with homes reduced to splinters. Material aid and heroic efforts on the part of rescue teams have made a difference, but the enormity of these catastrophes is, for most of us, beyond comprehension.

Particularly since 9/11, we have become at least somewhat inured to man-made crises and tragedies. We see images on TV and in the newspapers of the ongoing slaughter in Iraq, both of our troops and of innocent civilians. With barely a second glance, we pass over photos of wrecked trains, spewing deadly gas into small towns, or of children and the elderly dying of hunger in African war zones, or of handgun violence that takes the lives of our neighbors' teenagers. We have become so accustomed to man's inhumanity to man that these events sadden and trouble us, but they rarely shock us anymore.

It's quite another matter when outrageous damage and loss are produced by natural disasters. In the wake of the post-Christmas earthquake, the media conveyed devastating images: the corpses of more than a hundred little children laid side by side in a makeshift morgue; a father, with unspeakable agony etched in his face, bearing the lifeless body of his young son; a teenaged girl kneeling alone in the middle of a rubble strewn street, sobbing uncontrollably. . . . Of all these images, however, one of the most poignant was of a Christian pastor. He looked mournfully at the wreckage and carnage that lay all about him. Then he asked the interviewer, almost rhetorically: "How, in the face of all this, can we explain to people that God loves them, that God cares?"

This is a question many of us, victims and bystanders alike, have asked ourselves in these days. It's the age-old problem of "theodicy." How do we reconcile our image of a good, compassionate and all-powerful God with the reality of evil?

Muslim preachers were quick to lay blame for the disaster on the people's immorality: failure to follow the Quran's precepts, mingling with the infidels, imbibing alcohol, and premarital sex. To their mind, the tsunami, like other natural catastrophes, represents God's wrath wreaked upon sinful humanity. The image of God that underlies that conclusion, though, is radically different from the image Jesus offers us of His Father: a God of infinite power and sure justice, but also a God of mercy, compassion and unqualified love. A God who never inflicts indiscriminate slaughter, particularly on the innocent, as a matter of policy.

If there is any sense to be made of these tragedies from our poor, myopic perspective, it is one provided simply and eloquently by the Church's liturgical worship. From Nativity, through Theophany, and on to Holy Pascha, the common theme that we celebrate and proclaim to each other and to the world is summed up in the name given to Jesus at His birth, the name Emmanuel, "God is with us." This means not only that God accompanies us, remains present with us, and provides hope and consolation in our times of grief and loss. It means above all that God *shares* our suffering. He *takes part* in our pain and anguish, fully and to the bitter end. To put it somewhat melodramatically, yet accurately: with every drowned infant, every starving refugee, every family buried beneath a mudslide, and every fisherman lost in a "perfect storm," Christ the Son of God is present, and He suffers and weeps.

Since the high Middle Ages theologians have pondered the mystery of God's omniscience and omnipotence. In the process they have often lost sight of another aspect of divinity, one that for us is far more important. It is what the apostle Paul refers to as God's "kenotic" or self-emptying descent into the darkness and frailty of human life (Phil 2:7). Paul uses the word to speak of the incarnation of the Son of God, His taking flesh and becoming a human person, without ceasing to be God in His very essence. But, he declares, that kenotic descent does not end with Jesus' birth. For the Son of God further "humbled Himself and became obedient unto death, even death on a cross."

This is the distinguishing mark of Christianity. The quality that sets Christian revelation and Christian faith off from every form of religion is the one celebrated in the Church's worship. It is the truth that God's love for His people—for us—is such that He humbles and sacrifices Himself on our behalf. God suffers and dies, so that we might live in Him.

What does this mean about tsunamis, hurricanes, droughts and forest fires? First of all, that the incarnation of our Lord did not bring an end to cataclysmic natural disasters, any more than His resurrection brought an end to the process that leads to our physical death. That was not their purpose. Orthodox theology has always proclaimed that a vital if tragic link exists between ourselves and the cosmos, the created universe. In some inexplicable way, the cosmic order shares in and suffers from human sin, our rebellion against the God of life and love. Creation itself is caught up in "bondage to decay," "groaning in travail" until we ourselves attain the glorious fruits of redemption and adoption as children of God (Rom 8:20–23). In the meantime, as the apostle John tells us, "the whole world lies in [the power of] the Evil One" (1 Jn 5:19). If chaos is occasionally unleashed in the natural order, it is precisely because of this state of affairs: until God's work of salvation is complete, until our hope of redemption is finally fulfilled, evil will continue to impact our lives on both a human and a cosmic scale.

Another and still more important point, however, is the truth expressed in the name Emmanuel. In the midst of a critically unstable, and at times violently chaotic world, we can hold fast to the one truth, the one reality that matters: God is with us.

In this regard, we can say that the author of 1 Kings rather misunderstood the tradition he received concerning Elijah's experience on Mount Horeb (1 Kg 19). God was indeed present in the "still small voice." But He was also present in the wind, in the earthquake and in the fire. He was present then, He was present on December 26, 2004, He was present in the aftermath of Katrina, and He will be present until the very end. Present, but also knowing and sharing to the fullest extent the pain and anguish of all those who cry out from under the rubble.

2
Poker, R.I.P.

THE OTHER DAY WE HAD ONE OF our dogs put down, that is, euthanized. Actually, he wasn't even our dog. The neighbor had received him as a gift from his sister, had no interest in him, and neglected him completely, other than to toss a little food out to him in the evening. He was a beautiful animal, despite the matted hair, myriad ticks, and mud up to his tail from tramping through the marshes.

He was a thoroughbred English Spaniel, black and white, and gentle as a fawn. He had a fawn's eyes, too, large, liquid and a little sad. His owner had named him Poker. When the fellow said we could keep him, the poor animal was afflicted with heart worms, hook worms, ear mites and an eye infection. When we got him back from the vet, some $300 later, he clung to us so closely we began to call him Cody, for "co-dependent." But Poker he was, and Poker he remained.

The veterinarians, a man and a young woman, cared for Poker often during the three years he was ours. Last week, just before his tenth birthday, he stopped eating. Lethargy set in so that he could hardly get around. For a couple of days we nursed him at home, hoping it would pass. By the weekend, those deep, sad eyes told us we had to take him to the clinic. A blood test showed what we had feared: he had massive kidney failure. We could subject him to aggressive and painful treatment, the vet said, with no real chance of improvement. Or we could accept to put him to sleep. I thought about it, tried to pray about it—I loved this little creature—then called my wife, who drove up to join me.

The vets came in, both of them, and wrapped Poker in genuine affection. One of them pulled out a box of tissues in case we needed them. His eyes reddened, and he reached for one himself. Then the young woman, in a gesture of remarkable tenderness, inserted the needle, as I cradled Poker's head in my arms.

A moment later his heart stopped. The doctor touched his open eye with the tip of her finger and said quietly, "He's gone."

Gone where? She didn't say "He's dead," rather, "He's gone." Trying to hold back my own tears, my mind went back to the first time I carried a cadaver. It was in a small Swiss village, in 1968. An elderly friend named Paul, a leader in his local parish, died one morning in the shower. His wife, choked with grief, called the pastor, and he called me. We found Paul where he had fallen, lifted him up, carried him to the bed, and covered him to the chest with a sheet. I looked at him, and realized that he was "gone." Not dead, but simply gone, not there. This body stretched out on the bed was a shell, nothing more. Where was "Paul," the real Paul that we had known and loved? Like Poker, he was gone.

In the few minutes we stayed with Poker, who was warm yet lifeless, I thought too of the first meeting I had with Father Lev Gillet, the much-revered spiritual elder who wrote many brief and beautiful books under the name of "A Monk of the Eastern Church." It was the summer of 1967, and he and I, together with my wife and our infant son, were strolling down a street in London (he was for many years chaplain of the London-based Society of St Alban and St Sergius).

I don't recall how we got on the subject. I just remember Father Lev expressing the firm conviction that animals—particularly domestic animals who have lived with and been loved by people— experience some form of afterlife. He was a brilliant man, a highly respected theologian, whose writings on Scripture and Prayer of the Heart had offered spiritual nurture to multitudes of people throughout Europe and, to a lesser degree, in the United States. His words were not pious wishful thinking; they emerged from a life of thoughtful reflection and prayer.

Animals have an afterlife? At the time I couldn't quite believe it. Do animals have souls? And can those souls be what we call "eternal"?

If, like Father Lev, we can answer that question in the affirmative, it can only be by adjusting altogether our way of looking at God and His creation. He is the Creator and Lord of all, and in some special way, of every living thing. The mystic perceives heaven in a blade of grass, the petal of a flower, or a child's uplifted face. Heaven is not "out there." It's all around us, enveloping everything and everyone in light and beauty that once in a great while we can perceive as a gift of pure grace. And perceiving it, we enter into it, even in the midst of our daily routine, despite our distractions, despite our sin.

Everything that lives derives its life from God, from participation in the Life of God. In some inexplicable way, all living things come forth from God and return to Him. The life they share, again in some unfathomable and mysterious way, is God's own life. Perhaps this is what theologians mean by "panentheism": God is in and through all things, not ontologically as a pantheist would hold, but by grace—the dynamic and life-giving power of the Holy Spirit, "who is everywhere present, filling all things."

Is it conceivable that life simply disappears, ends, vanishes? Nothing vanishes, physicists tell us. If matter is transformed into energy, maybe something analogous occurs between the physical realm and the spiritual realm, between life and death. We know this happens with human persons, endowed with what we call an "immortal soul." A theologian would reply, "But persons are unique, made in the image of God." And my musings he would probably dismiss as nostalgic self-deception, a pointless and empty attempt to assuage the grief I feel over the loss of a little dog who used to cling to me like my shadow, a friend and companion whom I loved. Do dogs, too, have immortal souls? Does a blade of grass?

I can't answer these questions in any reasoned way, a way that is theologically convincing. All I can do is recall Father Lev's conviction that every creature finds its true destiny in the heart of the merciful God, because there it has its true origin. If God has shared our life in the person of Jesus, it is because we, from the moment of our creation, share His life. And that life is eternal. Is it permissible to make a logical leap here, to conclude that therefore not only our human life, but also every life, is likewise eternal?

I don't know. All I know is that I miss Poker, and somehow in my simple fantasy, I hope that he misses me. I hope that he is not dead, but that he is really "gone": gone home to the Creator of his life, that life that brought me warmth, laughter, love and occasional tears. I hope that for him, as for all of us, R.I.P. means not so much "Rest in Peace" as "Rejoice in Paradise." It's a naïve, childlike hope. And maybe it's vain, even heretical. But when I think of Poker—as when I think of our friend Paul, and everyone and everything that we love and cherish—I want very much for it to be a hope fulfilled.

3
Lest We Forget

> *Lord God of Hosts, be with us yet,*
> *Lest we forget—lest we forget!*
> —Rudyard Kipling, "Recessional"

*I*N 1999, THE ROMANIAN NATIONAL INSTITUTE for the Study of Totalitarianism published a volume entitled "The Imprisoned Church: Romania, 1944–1989." It is presented as a "dictionary" that details the persecution and suffering endured by clergy and other figures in the Orthodox, Catholic (Eastern and Roman) and Protestant Churches in Romania during the period of communist domination.

In his foreword to the volume, Dr Radu Ciuceanu states: "In just one year, 1922, the tragic balance sheet of the Russian Orthodox Church indicated 2,691 priests, 1,972 monks and 3,447 hermits had been assassinated. As the power was taken over by the Bolsheviks and terror was instated, the casualties multiplied."[1] The Dictionary goes on to give a thumbnail sketch of the persecution endured in Romania by more than 2,500 "ecclesiastical personnel," from the 1946 communist takeover until the Revolution of 1989. The following entries are typical:

---

[1]NIST publication of the Romanian Academy (Bucharest, 1999).

— Bogoevici, Pavel; Orthodox priest. Biography: Ministered at Bania; arrested in 1950; charge: sedition; sentenced to 12 years of correctional prison, detention places: Aiud, Turda, Gherla, The Canal; deceased.

— Bucur, Gheorghe; Orthodox priest. Biog: The communists took him to the Arges river, beat him up, threw him into the water, pulled on his beard, then let him surface and catch his breath just to torture him some more; deceased.

— Etdes, Stefan; Roman Catholic priest. He served in Lespezi, Bacau County; arrested for building the Parish Church.

— Paciu, Monica; Orthodox nun. Biog: Ministered at the Bistrita Monastery; beaten and raped by the *Securitate* [secret police] of Craiova; tried on 06.12.1949 by the Craiova Military Court.

— Stancu, Tinca; Orthodox nun. Biog: Sentenced by the Ploiesti Court to 1 year and 4 months imprisonment; charge: unauthorized wearing of uniform [the monastic habit], after the monastery she had belonged to was dismantled.

— Vasiliu, Mircea; Orthodox priest. Biog: Ministered at Roscani, Botosani county; detention place: Aiud; lung disease; abandoned without medical care, he died in that prison.

Similar entries exist for persons many of us know or have known over the years, persons whose spiritual, theological and pastoral witness has touched us deeply: Archimandrite Roman Braga, Fr Ilie Cleopa, Fr Dumitru Staniloae. . . .

Early in 2005, *The Orthodox Word* published a remarkable article by Nikolai Kolchurinsky, titled "Having Endured the Cross. The Martyric Death and Posthumous Miracles of Archpriest Constantine Podgorsky."[2] The author recounts the life and tragic death suffered by this new martyr of Russia, whose incorrupt relics have brought healing to multitudes of pilgrims. A priest in the village of Kirzhemany (Nizhni Novgorod), Father Constantine was serving the Divine Liturgy on November 7, 1918. Previously

[2]Vol. 41/1, no. 240 (Jan–Feb 2005): 33–41.

he had infuriated the revolutionary authorities by celebrating a *panikhida* (memorial service) for the Tsar Nicholas and his family, as well as by devoting himself unsparingly to the pastoral needs of his flock. On this day, he provoked the authorities still further by gathering his people for a festal Liturgy, while the revolutionaries expected the villagers to assemble for a celebration of the first anniversary of the Bolshevik rise to power.

Militants burst into the church during the following day's service, seized Fr Constantine and, tearing off his vestments, threw him into the street. After humiliating and torturing him, "they dragged the now weakened priest by the hair to the high church porch and crucified him on the church doors . . ."[3]

There have been other reports of priests being crucified in this way, by communists but also by representatives of non-Christian religions. Today, as we are all painfully aware, Christians are subjected to persecution, and at times execution, in numerous countries throughout the world. It's hackneyed but probably accurate to say that things will get worse before they get better. This is true in the United States, by the way, as well as in Saudi Arabia, Sudan or North Korea. When I was in seminary, back in the early 1960s, the society in general looked up to pastoral ministry as a noble profession, one that attracted bright, committed young people to a life of service and witness, coupled, for those who cared, with a certain degree of social status. Conditions nowadays have certainly not reverted to what they were under Stalin or Ceaucescu. But to commit oneself to seminary study and the pastoral ministry today requires far more courage, determination, and perhaps even faith, than it did in my day. And again, not only in the mission field and lands of Islamic fundamentalism, but here at home.

"The blood of the martyrs is the seed of the Church," Tertullian said. This is a truth we should neither forget nor minimize. The Epistle to the Hebrews closes with a recital of the sufferings borne by faithful Israelites in the period before Christ's coming. Since that time, countless martyrs and confessors have shared

[3]Ibid., 37.

directly, personally, in the sufferings of Christ. The cross they have endured is none other than the cross of Christ. And their cross, like His, is borne not so much for themselves as for us.

Their blood, mingled with the blood of Christ, nourishes the Church throughout the ages. For us, that commingled blood both assures us of what has been and presages what might lie ahead. Most of us will never go through the dread and suffering of martyrdom, but some will. And that fact alone tells us that in our prayer and our ecclesial consciousness, we must never forget the ultimate price paid by our Lord and by so many others in His name.

4
Hurricanes and Humming Birds

August 14, 2004. Hurricane Charley just came barreling through, lickety-split, hell-bent on more destruction up the Carolina coast. It already devastated a large swath of Florida, laying waste to the region around Port Charlotte. Several people were killed when their mobile homes went airborne, others were lost in the ruins of stores and office buildings, and the damage is estimated in the billions.

We got off easy. During the night, the rain and wind picked up to gale force. Branches came crashing down from the tops of pines and live oaks, carrying with them great soaked beards of gray-green Spanish moss. The road out of here that leads through the woods is under water, and the electricity went out a couple of hours ago. But we have food and water, and it's kind of nice to think that when the battery on this laptop gives out, I have a good excuse just to head for the dock and watch the tail end of the storm churn up the river. Considering that Charley is right now picking up speed and power as it sucks up heat from the coastal waters north of here, we really did get off easy.

As these things happen, the sun just came out. The sky suddenly turned deep blue on this Saturday morning, and except for the debris on the ground you'd never know that half an hour ago we were being battered by a hurricane.

All morning long the wind kept the bird feeders swinging so hard we thought they might become projectiles. (Next time a hurricane comes through your neighborhood, you might want to stow the things in the garage). Now, in an instant, the feeders are alive with cardinals, chickadees, red-winged blackbirds, titmice, buntings and a stray blue jay. The most striking sight, though, is the hummingbird feeder. Normally we spot only one or two of the little birds at a time, hovering like mini-helicopters while they gorge themselves on sugar-water. Right now a half dozen or more are fighting each other off to gain access to the red and yellow plastic flowers that provide them nourishment. It has been a long morning, what with the storm. These little creatures expend so much energy that they need to feed almost constantly. They're hungry and a little frantic. Their internal mechanisms had been telling them that if they didn't feed soon, they would die. They were completely at the mercy of the storm, their tiny, fragile bodies unable to withstand the gusts. They were forced to hunker down where they could, and wait. But then the storm passed and the sun came out.

Sometimes we are very much like those little humming birds. We find ourselves caught up in events or conditions that render us virtually helpless. I don't want to push the simile too far, but it's a fact that we often find ourselves in a storm that threatens our very existence. A pink slip appears in our In-box, or a frightening report comes back from the oncology lab; our teenager gets caught swapping drugs in school, or our spouse asks for a divorce. Or we're threatened by some natural disaster, such as a hurricane. On a less dramatic scale, we may be losing a battle with depression, or struggling to quit, once and for all, our daily intake of alcohol or nicotine. Each one of us can add to this list our own personal dramas: sins that threaten to do us in, or outside forces we have no control over, which make us, like those humming birds, hunker down and hope it will pass. In the meantime, we're hungry. And if we don't soon get the nourishment we need, we may starve to death.

Often it seems that God leads us to the very edge of the abyss before reaching out to rescue us. In times of crisis, self-imposed or inflicted from outside, we feel threatened and abandoned. Ages-old questions go through our minds: Where is God? Why does He allow this to happen? And why to me? Am I being punished for some known or unknown sin? Or does God just not care?

The great nineteenth-century philosopher-theologian Søren Kierkegaard gave an eloquent answer to questions like these. At the close of one of his "Edifying Discourses" he declared something like: "And so we may know that this same God, who by His hand led us through the world, now withdraws it . . . and opens His embrace to receive the longing soul."

In order to open that embrace, God must first let go of our hand. For a moment—one that feels like an eternity—He must withdraw His strength and support, and we feel abandoned. Yet God never abandons those He loves; and by an unfathomable miracle of grace, He loves us all.

It may be a stretched simile, this likening of our experiences to hurricanes and humming birds. But to those who have peered down into the abyss, or hunkered down in dread of abandonment and spiritual starvation, it may still apply. So while we wait for the storm to pass and the sun to come out, we can hold on tight to the assurance that Kierkegaard offered over a century and a half ago. If, for reasons beyond our comprehension, God withdraws His hand, it is only for a moment, so that He might open His arms to embrace our longing souls.

5
"What's the Difference?"

A SMALL GROUP OF A DOZEN OR SO young medical professionals were sitting around a table, munching cookies and downing soft drinks. They were all mainline Protestants or Evangelicals. Some were very much connected to their church tradition; others were thirsting for something else, which clearly meant something more. They had asked us to come and talk about Orthodoxy. Most of them had never been to an Orthodox worship service, and they were as curious as they were welcoming. Overall, the atmosphere was warm and cordial.

They raised the usual question: "What's the difference between your faith and ours, between the Orthodox and, say, Baptists?" Several of them had asked this kind of question to other Orthodox Christians, only to receive confusing and unsatisfying answers. Both priests and laypeople had given them the impression that the differences concerned either "things"—ecclesiastical trappings—or dogmas, usually wrapped up in obscure theological jargon. They had pointed to vestments, fasting, long services, incense, icons, and cupolas. Some had stressed the importance (and unavailability to the "heterodox") of Communion and Confession. Others had talked in more theological terms of the Orthodox view of the papacy and of the "filioque" clause added to the Nicene Creed. A few had focused on the interpretation of Romans 5:12 and the "transmission" of sin and guilt. And nearly all of them had denounced the Protestant notion of "Once saved, always saved," while they belittled long sermons, revivals and social activism.

People in the group looked at us and wanted to know if there wasn't more to it than that. For over two hours we exchanged thoughts about our respective beliefs and traditions. Finally we parted with warm handshakes, while a few asked if we could continue with this kind of exchange.

At home later that evening, I picked up the local paper and turned to the Religion section (a popular feature in Charleston, S.C., the "Holy City"). One column offered thoughts of two clergymen on the question of "miracle healings." What should a sick person do to receive one? An answer, provided by the pastor of the "Unity Temple on the Plaza" in Kansas City, contained an admission—a virtual confession of faith—that made me realize how inadequate my answers had been to questions raised earlier in the evening about the differences between Orthodoxy and other traditions. While most Protestants would not agree with this pastor's remarks, they are nevertheless representative of an overall attitude widespread in America's post-Christian culture.

"I don't believe that God intervenes in our lives," the good cleric wrote, "but I do believe that God Spirit [*sic*] is in every one of us, and the more we awaken to that power, the more we are able to utilize it for physical, emotional and mental healing." It reminded me of experiments recently undertaken by an atheistic professor at Harvard's medical school, to determine the usefulness of prayer for healing various illnesses.

What are the chief differences between Orthodoxy and other expressions of religious or, more specifically, Christian faith? It would take far more space than is available here to begin an adequate reply. There is one thing, though, that is too seldom talked about, yet seems to be among the most significant differences. That is the matter of perspective, of a worldview that beholds the presence, purpose and power of a loving and compassionate God, in all of creation and in every aspect of our personal life and experience. What does this mean for us and for our life in Christ?

Orthodox spiritual elders have often made the point that the uniqueness of Orthodoxy lies in its call to holiness: to a thorough-going transformation of the human person that leads to "the likeness of God." God intends that our life be a pilgrimage, an extraordinary adventure, that can lead progressively through stages of growth known in the monastic tradition as "purification," "illumination" and finally "deification": a real and eternal participation in the Life of the Holy Trinity. A quest for the likeness of God is a quest to be holy as our heavenly Father is holy, to strive not for our own perfection, but for His. It is to allow the Holy Spirit to re-create us in the Divine Image, to lead us from a self-centered state of sinfulness, corruption and death to one of righteousness, peace and joy, as we dwell in eternal and intimate communion with the Lord of all things.

Our Protestant colleagues are right: we can never make that kind of pilgrimage on our own. We can never attain holiness, never achieve sanctity, through our own actions or merits. Call it "salvation," or call it a quest for *theōsis* or "deification." In any case, the possibility and initiative lie wholly in the hands of God. If there is sanctification in this life, if there is any realistic hope for sharing in "eternal glory," it comes as a pure, undeserved and unearned gift.

In Orthodox experience, however, that gift is communicated to us in very specific ways, ordained by God Himself. These include entering into and making our own the Faith of our Fathers: the convictions about God and the human person that led many of those Fathers to sacrifice their lives rather than compromise their beliefs. They include active participation in the Body of Christ: its worship, its sacraments, and its self-giving service to God's world. This means that everything from vestments and incense to particular doctrinal positions have their place and their significance. Yet all "things," like all dogmas, serve a higher end. They serve our life and our growth, our pilgrimage, which leads toward the holiness that only God embodies and can convey.

The next time I share cookies and Coke with these Protestant friends, I hope I'll remember to begin and end where Orthodoxy itself begins and ends: with the notion of pilgrimage, of transformation and endless growth in the Spirit. Bishop Kallistos Ware began his marvelous little book *The Orthodox Way* with the story of an old woman who lived as a recluse in Rome. Asked by St Serapion why she spent her time just sitting in her room, she replied, "I am not sitting. I am on a journey."

If we are to behold the presence and power of God in our life and in all creation, it can only be by embarking on just that kind of journey. For those who do—who take up, with faith and love, an ardent quest for holiness—their very life reveals the most significant differences that set Orthodoxy apart from other expressions of faith (including nominal Orthodoxy). Their life becomes a powerful witness that draws others into the same pilgrimage, the same adventure of faith and love, that they themselves are on. And more than the splendor of vestments or the beauty of liturgical music, more than any persuasive arguments about doctrine and ecclesial praxis, that witness will lead others to move beyond the differences and toward an appreciation of Orthodoxy in its essence and at its heart.

6

What They Didn't Teach Me in Seminary

THE PHONE RANG RIGHT AT SUPPERTIME. A hysterical voice on the other end started berating me for not listening to her, for abandoning her in her most dire need, for not really hearing her confession, for being self-centered and abusive toward her and everyone else in the parish. No, rather it was the parish community itself, those egotistical, ungrateful people, who had abandoned her, offended her, tried to set limits they knew she couldn't accept.

This was the third call from her in the past twenty-four hours. Supper was getting cold, and my wife was becoming less and less patient. For several months she had put up with invasive calls from this same person and was getting tired of it. Finally I broke it off and told the person not to call my home again. If she wanted to talk, if she wanted to hear my recommendations—which included her getting therapy—then she should make an appointment, and I would be glad to do whatever I could. There was a loud click, and I never heard from her again. Shortly thereafter she went back to the Catholic Church, which she had stormed out of several years earlier, largely, it seems, because the local priest had responded to her demands much as I did myself.

For a long while afterwards I felt awful. She had succeeded in laying a heavy guilt trip on me: true to form, I had "abandoned," "rejected," and "insulted" her, "like all priests do to their spiritual children," she insisted. She was actually becoming a wedge between my wife and me, and I was allowing it to happen. Should I have yelled at her to go get help? Or continued to sympathize with her only to reinforce her co-dependency? Or given up, and opened a grocery store somewhere downtown?

Why didn't they teach me about things like this in seminary?

Last month the *starosta* and choir director got into a squabble that threatened to turn into a fight. It ended peacefully enough, but the finale was hardly amicable. Then a couple of days later one of our people heard of a great offer for a used van. She had often urged the parish council to provide transportation for youth outings, so she took the bait, signed papers with a local used car salesman in the name of the parish, and (generously) made a first payment out of her own pocket. In addition to a leaking roof, mortgage outlays on the education building and a horrendous problem with termite control, we now have payments to make on a ten-year-old van that gets twelve miles to the gallon.

Why didn't somebody warn me about these kinds of things when I was in seminary?

One of our young priests phoned the other day. He's exceptionally dedicated and conscientious as well as being very bright. He sounded both distressed and depressed. One of his aged, ailing parishioners was on life-support in the local hospital. The medical team, the hospital ethics committee and several family members felt the old man was struggling to die and that consequently he should be taken off the ventilator. The priest agreed. Two of the man's daughters, however, were determined to draw every breath from him they could. "You people," including the priest, they argued, "are simply trying to get rid of him!" Take him off life-support, they yelled, and we'll sue every one of you for wrongful death—beginning with the priest, since he was supposed to be the moral arbiter.

After he told me all this, he added plaintively: "Why didn't they teach me how to handle this kind of situation when I was in seminary?"

These may be exaggerated (albeit real) situations, but they call up a familiar theme. Why don't seminary courses provide us with ways and means to deal with such common crises as these? A cynical answer would be that seminary faculty members avoid dealing with matters like this out of fear that if they do, none of the students will go into the priesthood. . . . But that's unfair. And it's also wrong.

The point is, there are a great many aspects of priestly ministry that can be learned only by direct experience in a parish context. Our newly introduced seminary intern programs provide invaluable experience in this regard, and they need to be expanded; *massively* expanded, so that every one of our future clergy, and anyone—ordained or not—who will be working, praying and otherwise dealing with people on a close, personal basis, can profit from this vital aspect of seminary education. Similar programs need to be developed and funded for clergy already in the field, to give them experience with a broad variety of situations in which fragile, sinful human behavior threatens the well-being of our parishioners and parish communities.

Seminaries are not equipped to offer training in dealing with such daily realities as co-dependency, obsessive-compulsive disorders, or the panic and grief that so often accompany the impending death of a loved one. Courses in pastoral counseling and bioethics, for example, can offer valuable information and insight. But seminaries are simply not made to deal with many of the critical issues that occupy, preoccupy and often distress our clergy and others in the Church who hold some form of pastoral responsibility.

Perhaps in addition to a father confessor, each of our priests needs an experienced elder—a practiced and spiritually sensitive priest or layperson—who can serve as a more or less official mentor. Even if the person doesn't have all the answers (and nobody does), the possibility to talk on a regular basis with someone we trust, for whom we feel a certain affection and respect, goes a long way toward easing stress and providing pastorally appropriate answers to crises in ministry.

What we should be taught in seminary, in addition to normal course content, is that each of us needs another member of the Body of Christ to offer us a renewed vision of authentic priesthood.[4] This means someone with whom we can share—in total confidence and confidentiality—the problems we face, both personal and pastoral, knowing that this person continues to pray for us, and remains available to listen and to hear what we are saying. (Ideally this would in fact be our spiritual father; but restraints on his time and other factors may make it necessary for us to seek out someone to complement his ministry to us.) In brief, each of us, laity as well as clergy, needs an older brother or sister in Christ, who knows us, cares for us, and offers us in daily prayer to the guidance and the mercy of God.

No seminary curriculum can provide this kind of support. It is a matter of personal relationship, of friendship and love. It is a priceless gift that only God can offer to us, one for which we can and should pray without ceasing, until it becomes ours.

---

[4]Father Lev Gillet, also known as the "Monk of the Eastern Church," was just such a spiritual guide. An extraordinary amount of wisdom is contained in his simple essay written for clergy, entitled "Be My Priest," in *Serve The Lord With Gladness* (Crestwood, N.Y.: St Vladimir's Seminary Press, 1990).

7

On Casting Stones

A DEVASTATING CARTOON APPEARED RECENTLY in our local paper. The caption reads: "The New Sacrament." It depicts a somber and stately Episcopal church, with stained glass windows and cathedral roof. The view is from the back of the altar area, looking out toward the nave. Several small, robed figures surround a cleric, who is garbed all in white. According to the inscription on his vestments, he represents "U.S. Episcopal Bishops."

We see the scene from behind, so the figures are turned away, facing the congregation. An open service book, a cross, and two cruets, for wine and water, are to the bishop's left; a chalice stands to his right. It is the moment of the Elevation of the Host. The bishop's hands are lifted high above his head, raising the object of veneration. On the uplifted Host are inscribed the words, "Anything Goes!"

This may be a depiction of the "new sacrament" in the Episcopal Church. Then again, it may represent a bitter reaction to what has long characterized Anglican tradition: an openness to new things—movements, ideas, trends—with a genuine (if misguided) concern to be all-inclusive, to embrace all peoples, with their vast spectrum of theological and moral perspectives. As long as the faithful, with their clergy and theologians, respect the Gospel's first commandment to love the neighbor, whoever she or he may be, then according to this perspective, other matters, particularly of faith and morals, can be left to the individual believer.

In such an ecclesial world, the only unacceptable theological perspective holds that heresy exists.

All of this came to a head in 2003, when the Episcopal House of Bishops confirmed the election of an actively homosexual priest to be bishop of a New England diocese. That gesture deeply divided Episcopalians, setting modernists against traditionalists, with the risk of sundering their Church in this country and throughout the world.

It would be—and has been—easy for us as Orthodox Christians to point an accusatory finger, to condemn outright what we take to be a gross if not fatal misstep on the part of ecclesiastical authorities, and to dismiss the Episcopal Church as hopelessly beyond the pale. We can not and should never follow the path they have taken. That to most of us, I suppose, is self-evident. But we need to avoid the path of the Pharisee as well.

Perhaps the most appropriate emotional response we as Orthodox Christians can have to these and similarly distressing developments in the Episcopal Church is one of sadness. If it were not for Anglican friends in England and throughout Western Europe, the Russian communities of the diaspora, in the years following the October Revolution, would likely have faced insurmountable difficulties establishing their own churches and providing for theological education. The Anglican-Orthodox Fellowship of St Alban and St Sergius in London served to create bonds of unity and provide material aid that permitted the founding of numerous Orthodox parish churches and the continued life and work of the St Sergius Theological Institute in Paris. Independently and through the World Council of Churches, the Anglican Communion provided our forebears with invaluable help, together with countless signs of friendship and love.

But I think especially of those in the Episcopal Church today, who are suffering in ways we can hardly imagine, because of the direction their ecclesial authorities are taking them. It would be easy, and fatuous, to say: "Well, let them become Orthodox!" Many of them were born and raised in a tradition they love and cherish. All their life they have prayed, sung and served in their Church. And now their Church seems to have been taken hostage by forces alien to what they have known, trusted, respected and honored. As they put it: they have not left the church; the church has left them.

Together with these people—who love Christ and are deeply loved by Him—there are those we more easily criticize, even condemn, as responsible for the present turmoil. Yet here, too, as was evident in the debates in the Episcopal House of Bishops, there is genuine concern to follow God's will and remain faithful to the gospel. We may disagree radically with their interpretation of Scripture and the actions they have taken. Yet we need to appreciate that the motivation behind their actions was a sincere concern to minister effectively to an entire class of people who, for good reasons or bad, have been essentially marginalized.

Yes, the road to hell is paved with good intentions. Yet it remains true that the vote in the House of Bishops reflects an aspect of the gospel of Christ that we tend too often to neglect. This is Christ's call to minister to outcasts, whatever the reasons for their behavior or their infirmity. How often was He criticized for fraternizing with tax collectors, prostitutes, the blind, the demon-possessed, and others who were deemed worthy only of divine wrath?

Our Episcopal brothers and sisters are going through a struggle today that we, mercifully, have been spared, at least until now. In the Orthodox Church we have our own issues with homosexual behavior, and we mustn't forget that. Just as we are called to minister to our own, whatever their sexual orientation and behavior, we are called to serve those of other communions, or of none. In this respect, at least, we are called as well to honor the motivation of many in authority within the Episcopal Church: not simply to pander to the "gay agenda," but to accept every person as a bearer of the Image of God.

Rather than cast stones, then, may we implore God's mercy upon the Episcopal fold. May we offer them up, like the eucharistic Host, with the earnest desire that God will grant them healing. And may we pray for them as for ourselves, that we be faithful to the life and faith to which God calls us, for our own salvation and the salvation of all His people, whoever they may be.

8
"All I Gotta Do"

THE LITTLE BOX OF CDs WEDGED BETWEEN the front seats of our car contains labels such as "Mozart's Piano Concertos 18 & 19," "The Vigil service of the Kiev Monastery," "Tomaso Albinoni's Cantatas from Opus 4," and "The Best of the Beach Boys." ("That's Daddy," my kids sigh, rolling their eyes toward heaven.)

When I'm tired or on a long trip, though, I usually forego this heavy stuff and tune in to Charleston's "Cat Country!" at "107.5 on yo' dahl." Tim McGraw (yeah, and Faith Hill!), Alan Jackson and "Alabama"—that kind of thing. I'm not sure why this appeals to me, besides the fact that it churns up the decibels that keep me from drifting off at the wheel. I think it has to do with the pop philosophy that every once in a while lifts country music to nearly sublime heights.

There's one line from the group "Alabama" that comes back to me, maybe too often. It's a lament for our time, a plaintive cry of resistance and caving in, which expresses both fatalism and frustration in a world that's out of control.

"All I gotta do is live and die, / But I'm in a hurry an' I don't know why . . ."

I recall the first time I visited a Trappist monastery, located in a remote area between Normandy and Brittany on the north coast of France. A Catholic friend introduced me to an elderly monk, dressed in white shirt and black pants, who was coming out of the ancient stone chapel. The office was over. He had laid aside his cowl and was coming back to the little building near the monastery entrance, where he welcomed visitors. He was subdued, yet radiant. There was a quiet peace about him that you could almost touch and see, an aura of gentle holiness that set him apart from the rest of us.

For the next few hours he would sit in that tiny space, thinking, praying and exploring his own inner space, as he waited for pilgrims to pass by. We talked for a few minutes, and I learned that this is what he did virtually every day. Two hours before dawn reading and meditating in his cell, six to eight hours in the chapel, four in his little welcoming hut, one or two in the refectory and chapter, then a little time for sleep. Whatever was left over, usually two or three hours a day, he spent working on the grounds, cleaning up after guests, pulling stray weeds, and watching the wildlife.

All the time his inner space was attuned to higher things: beautiful, transcendent things that suffused his entire being with a quiet joy and often brought him to tears. He didn't tell us this last part; we learned it from our friend, who had known him from childhood.

The world is filled with souls like this Trappist monk. To many of us, their routine would be a mind-numbing waste of time. They don't DO anything! They are willfully, wantonly, scandalously unproductive. All they've got to do is live and die. And to what end?

All I've got to do, too, is live and die. All God asks of me, and all of us, is to assume the stewardship of our life, acknowledge that we belong to Him and owe our entire being to Him, and then die in peace, in His time and in the way He intends. That's all.

But I'm in a hurry, and I don't know why. I'm driven by some odd compulsion that makes me feel I've always got to *do* something: to perform, accomplish, create, whatever. I've bought in to the competitor-consumer mentality of the world I live in, and I can't ever do enough to buy my way out. If I make more money, achieve some goal (usually suggested by somebody else), work hard enough to merit a few strokes from those above me, or simply keep busy enough so I don't feel guilty at knocking off for a few hours, then my life is worth while, then I've succeeded.

But of course I can't ever win that frantic race. It's not just because there are too many others ahead of me. It's because I'm in the wrong race to begin with.

"Take time to smell the roses," they tell us. No, take time to plant, cultivate and cherish those roses. Take time to make warfare against frenetic activity and compulsive over-achievement, time to take stock of values and virtues long lost in the dust of "doing things."

Take time like that Trappist monk, to pray, meditate and think. Take time to wonder at the beauty of creation, to welcome those who pass through the gates of your daily experience, to "sing a new song" (Ps 33:2–4) from the depths of your heart to the One who calls us to live and to die in Him, filled with His peace, His love and His purpose.

All this I say to myself, knowing full well that I barely listen. Yet every once in a while I can turn off Mozart or McGraw, slow down and just *be*. Then, somehow, I'm no longer hurrying about madly in a meaningless world, no longer just living to die. Somehow, for a few minutes at least, I'm able to hear and appreciate St Paul's words, addressed to Christians living in the noise, the busyness and the stress of ancient Rome: "If we live, we live to the Lord, and if we die, we die to the Lord. So then, whether we live or whether we die, we are the Lord's" (Rom 14: 7–9).

9

Church Billboard Slogans

ONE OF MY WORST PASSIONS IS irritation and one of my worst irritations is church billboard slogans. I don't know why these things bother me so much, but they do.

Between the Piggly Wiggly grocery store on the Maybank Highway, some ten miles north of here, and the Rockville, S.C., "yacht club" the same distance south, there are about twenty-five churches. Most, I suspect, have been incorporated to avoid land taxes; you almost never see a car parked out front, not even on Sunday mornings. Some of them, though, are thriving congregations whose parking lots are crammed full half the nights of the week (if only they were Orthodox . . .). While driving past, it's all but impossible not to read the inspirational inscriptions posted on their display boards. And they're not alone. There are other examples of this kind of ecclesial infomercial scattered all up and down the Maybank, from Folly Road just south of Charleston to the end of Bear's Bluff on Wadmalaw Island. Here are just a few, selected at random.

The Book of Acts Church, just a stone's throw from the local True Value Hardware, recently attempted to lure passing motorists with this startling example of Johannine exegesis: "Jesus is the Bread of Life. Come on in and have a slice!" (A friend spotted a variant on this theme somewhere out of town: "Without the Bread of Life, you're burnt toast!").

215

An explicitly Southern Methodist Church a little farther on offers a rather in-your-face bit of advice as gnats and July weather advance on the lowcountry: "Don't like the heat? Prepare to avoid it!" It's pretty clear they're not talking about summer escapes to the Blue Ridge Mountains.

An AME church on Bear's Bluff Road assures us that "God answers knee-mail!" And some congregation I can't quite recall lowered the bar with this nonsequitur: "Suffering from truth decay? Brush up on your Bible!"

It took a minute of soulful reflection to get the point of this one, but the paschal consolation was worth it: "Body piercing saved our life!"

Maybe the worst, from a strictly theological point of view, was posted on a large panel in front of a very large parish building, located on the north end of the Maybank beyond the Wappoo Cut, where nobody who lives on the barrier islands could miss it. I'd seen it in a few places before, but the absurdity—and tragedy—of its message hit me especially hard as I was coming home one night after giving a talk on the Holy Trinity. The message was a threat, couched in attempted humor: " 'Don't make me come down there!'—God."

It's not only the Islamists and assorted Unitarians who make me wonder if we all worship the same God. It's also my neighbors who put up with a pastor who would post that kind of thing outside his church.

I was tempted to duct tape a piece of cardboard to the base of the panel, offering the corrective: "I did come down there, but there was nobody home!" This was to be a cleverly veiled allusion to the prologue of St John's Gospel. Fortunately, better sense led me to keep my nonsense to myself and drive on (leaving an Orthodox response to our priest, who handled it very well).

Instead of bromides and heresies, why can't some of these "Bible churches" post words from their more splendid hymns? Something along the lines of "The heavens are telling the glory of God," or even "Just as I am, without one plea, O Lamb of God, I come to Thee!"

I really don't much like church billboard slogans. But every once in a while something appears on one of those ubiquitous display panels that puts me to shame and teaches me not to judge—especially not to judge my Christian brother.

Remember the Book of Acts church and its invitation to take a slice of the Bread of Life? It's located in an area that's still scarred by a lot of rural poverty. Last time I passed that church the message had changed, even though the idea behind it hadn't. In place of the cute bit of Johannine exegesis, it said simply: "Free summer lunch, 12:00 noon."

10

Tithing: Putting God to the Test

Every good and perfect gift is from above . . .
Thine own of Thine own, we offer Thee.
—The Orthodox Liturgy

*I*T IS A MORAL AND SPIRITUAL IMPERATIVE for Orthodox Christians to consecrate to God *all* of their wealth and possessions—together with their very life—for His purpose and to His glory. This imperative was given concrete expression by the Old Testament commandment to offer tithes: one tenth of produce and livestock was consecrated to the Lord in imitation of Abram's offering of a tenth of the spoils of war to Melchizedek, "priest of God Most High" (Gen 14:19–20; cf. Lev 27:30–33; Num 18). In practice, Israel's tithes provided material support for the Temple and its priests. With the Deuteronomic reform, the tithe was extended to offer support as well for Levites (who held no property), sojourners, widows and orphans (Deut 14:27–29).

In the early Church, the act of tithing became a symbol of the gift of oneself as well as of one's possessions, offered to God as a gesture of thanksgiving and love (cf. *Didachē* 13:7: ". . . of all your possessions, take the firstfruits . . . and give according to the commandment"; St Irenaeus, *Against Heresies* IV.18.1: "The oblation of the Church, which the Lord gave instructions to be offered throughout all the world, is received by God as a pure sacrifice . . .

[H]e who offers is himself glorified in what he offers, if his gift is accepted"; St John Chrysostom, *Hom. in Eph.* II, passim).

In Deuteronomy 14:22f, tithes are offered and consumed in the context of a sacrificial meal. Although the Church never developed in any formal sense the relation between tithing and the eucharistic meal (the Divine Liturgy does nevertheless invoke God's blessing on "those who remember the poor"), this Old Testament link between the gift and the meal suggests that tithing possesses a *sacramental* quality.

As Orthodox Christians living in an excessively competitive society, in which Mammon is the god of choice, we need to recover this sacramental aspect of tithing as a symbolic offering of "all our life to Christ, our God." Tithing is less an economic issue than a spiritual one. It is not just a means to support programs and ministries of the institutional Church. Its true purpose is to acknowledge, in the most concrete and visible way possible, that God is absolute Sovereign over our life, and that our faith in Him—and in His faithfulness—signifies absolute trust in His promises (Mt 6:19–34!).

It's in this perspective that I would like to make the following proposal, one that has proven its worth in parts of the Diocese of the South and elsewhere: That the Orthodox Church in America, together with other jurisdictions, undertake a major program to educate our faithful in the spiritual as well as practical necessity to tithe of their material goods, particularly by dedicating at least one tenth of their annual income to the programs and ministries of the institutional Church and to favorite charities. This educational program can be carried out through Bible study, Christian education and preaching in the local parishes; through the curriculum of our seminaries that would include a focus on problems of wealth and poverty; and through statements by our bishops to encourage the faithful to return to the practice of tithing in accordance with biblical teaching.

To aid in this educational process, the Fellowship of Orthodox Stewards (FOS) might consider creating a new category of commitment, based on a tithe of one's total (net) income. The Church might propose, for example, that over a fixed period (one to three years, to begin with), our Orthodox faithful agree to make a sacrificial offering of 10% of their income, of which half would be specifically devoted to institutions of the Church (the parish, the diocese, the chancery) and the other half to special needs within the Church (IOCC, OCMC, Project Mexico, seminary and other appeals, and so forth.), or to favorite charities (cancer research, food banks) and social projects (Habitat for Humanity, pro-life activities) which aim to alleviate human poverty and misery.

If accepted by even a relatively small percentage of our people, this initiative would help dramatically in meeting the financial needs of our Church institutions, programs and ministries. And it would produce spiritual fruit of the greatest importance, as Orthodox Christians come to experience the truth of the Russian proverb: "The hands of those who give are always full." God Himself spoke this assurance millennia ago, through the voice of the prophet Malachi (3:6–11).

The people, Malachi declares, rob the Lord by not bringing the full tithes into the storehouse of the Jerusalem Temple. God responds: "Bring the full tithes into the storehouse, that there may be food in my house; and thereby *put me to the test*, says the Lord of hosts, if I will not open the window of heaven for you and pour down for you an overflowing blessing!"

11
Seeing Is Believing

JESUS URGED HIS DISCIPLES TO open their eyes to the world around them and behold the hand of God. In the seasons of the year, in the gathering of storms, in the birds of the air and flowers of the field, signs are offered that reveal God's presence and purpose. Those who have eyes that perceive deeper things can discover that divine presence in Jesus' own person and in the radiance of His own face. "He who has seen me," He tells Philip, "has seen the Father" (Jn 14:9). In order to believe the other disciples' witness, the apostle Thomas needs to *see* the risen Lord. Once that vision is granted to him, his hope is fulfilled and his joy is complete.

In this same vein, the Fathers of the Church declared that the ultimate purpose of reading Scripture is to acquire *theōria*, an inspired "vision" of God and His Truth. We read the Word of God and we hear it proclaimed through preaching and liturgical hymns. Yet we never really grasp it, understand it and take it into ourselves until we can "see" it—that is, until the words become in some sense icons, sacred images that enable written words to become a living Word. In order for the biblical text to be heard, it also needs to be seen. It needs to convey to us visual impressions that imprint themselves on our memory. Like Thomas, once we have actually beheld Christ, through the Scriptures and in our personal experience, then we can truly believe.

The other day a friend was lamenting the difficulty he found in discovering God's presence in the midst of his daily routine. With war raging in Iraq, with images of the horrors being perpetrated by all sides in the world's vast number of conflicts, with anxieties growing over gas prices and tuition costs, and with natural disasters multiplying around the globe, he has a hard time perceiving through the fog any trace of divine presence and purpose, and still less of beauty and holiness. All the earthly cares that impact upon him each day become distractions that get in the way of his prayer and numb him to any goodness and beauty that may actually lie about him. He is more discouraged and worried than depressed. That is, his condition is more spiritual than psychological. And he's looking for something else, something more than what's offered in the paper or on CNN or by the water cooler at work.

I didn't have much to say, because I find myself in that state sometimes, too. What strikes me, though, is that the state itself is most appropriately characterized as blindness. I don't any longer see what I know to be true. I can read about it in Scripture, even celebrate it in a church service. But if I'm not able to behold it, to perceive its reality and truth with the eyes of the heart, then it might just as well not exist. Like Philip and Thomas, we need to look beyond what is immediately present and see reality in its depths. Then we can enter into it and make it our own. It's the difference between looking into a fish tank and swimming amid coral reefs, between mowing the lawn and picking wildflowers, between passing a school playground and holding a young child in your lap. We can look at good and beautiful things, or we can truly *see* them. And when we do see them, then we see beyond them, into a deeper reality. We can see in a Bible story the living Word of God, and in the person of Jesus, the very face of the Father.

In an effort to make this point, I shared with my friend a little piece of verse from many years ago. It's not intended to be [auto]biographical. It grew out of an encounter with a person who, in total simplicity and humility, radiated holiness. Most people around him, it seems, never saw anything special in him at all. If

I was allowed to perceive in and beyond him something that touched my life to the core, it had nothing to do with me; it came as a gift of grace. The point is, once again, that if we have eyes to see, as every one of us can have, then we perceive miracles all about us. The birds of the air and the lilies of the field become signs of Heaven, and holy people give irrefutable proof of the presence, the power, the majesty and the glory of God.

The Hermitage

Nothing ever happens here—
No miracles attract the eye,
No interviewer questions why
He chose to live so very near
To nowhere. Tourists never come
Encroaching on his solitude.
No neighbors ever bring him food
Or seek him out for fun as some
Eccentric curiosity.
They sense his need to be alone,
And so they leave him on his own
To dwell in dull obscurity.

Nothing ever happens here—
No crises ever change the pace
That marks this simple, quiet place.
No would-be pilgrims flock to hear
Him sing the sacred liturgy
He offers up with fervent tears
Within this forest chapel. Years
Pass by, yet no one comes to see
What I have seen: that when he stands
To consecrate the holy bread
A dazzling light surrounds his head
And flames leap from his outstretched hands!

12
The Place of the Heart

"GOD REVEALS HIMSELF IN THE SILENCE OF THE HEART." The early desert monks, followed by ascetic laborers of every generation, came to know this truth through their own, most personal experience.

We can acquire knowledge about God in many different ways, first of all through the Bible and the Liturgy. The question, however, is how we move from knowledge *about* God to knowledge *of* God, that is, to an ever-deepening communion with Him in love.

This is a critical question, especially when we find ourselves overwhelmed by some crisis or tragedy in our life that strains our capacity to believe. The same question arises, though, whenever we attempt to respond to some inner longing to know God personally and intimately. That longing is a gift that God bestows on us, one that corresponds to His longing for communion with us. As a contemplative Catholic sister once told me, "God has placed an insatiable longing for Himself in the depths of every human heart."

The ascetic tradition tells us that such longing is met and satisfied at the core of our being, in the inner recesses of what the Psalmist calls "the secret heart" (Ps 50/51). After Holy Friday vespers some years ago I was in the kitchen of one of our monasteries, eating toast and drinking a cup of tea with an elderly priest who had spent many years in prison during the period of Communist rule in Romania. His only offense had been to preach the gospel and serve the people God had entrusted to him. We spoke a little about spiritual trials, and he alluded to those years and to their brutality. His eyes betrayed his emotion as he recalled the loneliness and the pain he had endured. For a few minutes he was quiet. Then he slowly made the sign of the cross and said, "I thank God for those years. . . . Because they made me go inside."

"They made me go inside." This man, and so many like him, could have given up to despair. Instead, by the mercy of God, he was able to enter the depths of his own being, the temple of the heart. That prison, with its bitter hardship and persecution, its loneliness and grief, was transformed into a spiritual desert. There he was able to engage in warfare with demons both within and without, and he emerged from it strengthened and renewed.

The thread that binds his experience with the intuition of the Catholic sister is their common focus on the heart. As holy people within the Body of Christ have always known, it is there that God most fully reveals Himself. After earthquake, wind and fire, it is there that His still small voice speaks ineffable words of consolation and peace. This is as true for us, in the ordinary routine of our daily lives, as it is for a Father Arseny,[5] a Mother Elisabeth,[6] and all those who have suffered immensely, knowing they were bearing the Cross of Christ.

True knowledge of God is experiential. Reading the Holy Scriptures and spiritual writings, participating regularly in liturgical worship, devoting ourselves to works of love: these are indispensable if we are to acquire such knowledge. Yet much depends on our ability to read, pray and serve at the level of the heart.

To enter into that sacred space, in this culture and with the usual demands on our time and energy, is no easy matter. We may try to pray each day, read through the Prayer Book prayers, or

---

[5]*Father Arseny, 1893–1973: Priest, Prisoner, Spiritual Father*, trans. Vera Bouteneff (Crestwood, N.Y.: St Vladimir's Seminary Press, 1998).

[6]The Grand Duchess of Russia and martyred monastic.

open the Bible for a few minutes, all in an effort to come into God's presence, as though God were "out there" and had to be invited or coerced to enter our life. We forget that the heart is more than a physical organ. It is a temple, where the Holy Spirit dwells with grace and power. Our task is to enter the space of the heart, to descend into its sacred depths, and to stand in humble awe before Him.

To make that inner journey, it is sometimes necessary to put aside books, liturgical tapes, even the Bible, and to spend a few moments in silence. The early morning or the evening after dark are good times to go into our room, close the door, and light a candle before an icon. There in that stillness we can collect ourselves and focus on what is most important in our life. We can make our confession, begging God's merciful forgiveness for our sins and shortcomings. We can offer up in thanksgiving the gifts of family and friends, of achievements and healings that we have received by His grace. We can make intercession, begging His mercy and healing for ourselves and for those we love, for our enemies and for all the people of His world. In that silence we can also allow Him to speak to us and to make Himself known.

Prayer of the heart is more than an oft-repeated formula, more than a confession of faith and an appeal for mercy. The traditional words, "Lord Jesus Christ, have mercy on me!" have extraordinary power. They possess the power of the Name of the Son of God, which "upholds the universe" (*Shepherd of Hermas* IX.14.5). Those words, however, like all prayers, find their most true and powerful expression when they flow from the heart, from the depths of inner silence.

We strive to move from knowledge about God to communion with Him. This striving, which arises from an insatiable, divinely bestowed longing, leads us finally to the place of the heart. Miraculously, in the stillness of that place and in the presence of the Holy, we enter, for a moment at least, into Paradise.

13

Prayer of the Heart

T HERE SEEMS TO BE AN UNBRIDGEABLE GAP between the richness of Orthodox tradition regarding "prayer of the heart" and the poor prayer that is part of our personal experience. Prayer of the heart requires *hēsychia*, a deep inner stillness that permits us to hear "the still small voice of God" (1 Kg 19:12). Is that really within our reach today, given the conditions of stress, overwork and dispersion that so mark our daily life?

Most of traditional hesychast teaching was formulated by ascetic elders and transmitted to younger monks. It is a tradition developed in the monastery and aimed principally at monastic life. Its roots, however, go back to the New Testament and to Jesus' own teaching and experience.

Frequently the Gospels show Jesus separating Himself for a while in order to pray to His Father in secret. Then to His prayer there is joined that of others, persons who supplicate either Him or God the Father for mercy and forgiveness. "Jesus, Son of David, have mercy on me!" cries the blind beggar Bartimaeus (Mk 10:47). In Jesus' parable of the Publican and the Pharisee (Lk 18:9ff), the publican or tax collector cries from the depths of his misery, "O God, have mercy on me, a sinner!" Gradually, appeals such as these gave rise to the familiar formula of the Jesus Prayer, "Lord Jesus Christ, Son of God, have mercy on me, a sinner."

Throughout history, and perhaps especially in our own day, this prayer or some variant of it has served as the cornerstone of the prayer and worship of laypersons as well as monastics. Hesychasm, in other words, is not the product of a medieval controversy between Athonite monks and Latin theologians, as some have argued. It is an ancient yet living tradition that anyone, with proper spiritual guidance, can seek to internalize and experience as a primary means for creating and maintaining a deep, personal and unbroken communion with God.

"Let the remembrance of Jesus [that is, the Jesus Prayer] be present with each breath," St John of Sinai urges his monks, "and then you will know the value of solitude."[7] St Hesychios the Priest, recalling these words of St John, adds, "Lash the enemy with the name of Jesus and, as a certain wise man has said, let the name of Jesus adhere to your breath, and then you will know the blessings of stillness."[8]

Those blessings have been admirably described by Nikitas Stithatos in his treatise entitled "On the Inner Nature of Things."[9]

> Stillness is an undisturbed state of the intellect, the calm of a free and joyful soul, the tranquil unwavering stability of the heart in God, the contemplation of light, the knowledge of the mysteries of God, consciousness of wisdom by virtue of a pure mind, the abyss of divine intellections, the rapture of the intellect, intercourse with God, and unsleeping watchfulness, spiritual prayer, untroubled repose in the midst of great hardship and, finally, solidarity and union with God.

Where do these glimpses into the hesychast tradition lead us? Is it really possible for us today, as monastics, clergy or laypeople, to acquire the gift of ceaseless prayer, to sound the depths and scale the heights of pure prayer?

---

[7] The Ladder of Divine Ascent Step 27.61 (trans. Archim. Lazarus Moore [London: 1959], 246).

[8]"On Watchfulness," The Philokalia, vol. 1 (London: Faber & Faber, 1995), 179.

[9] The Philokalia, vol. 4 (London: Faber & Faber, 1995), 125.

If we consider the lives of holy people such as St Silouan of Mount Athos, or Father Arseny (Streltzov) of the Soviet gulag, or countless lay men and women who make at least occasional use of the Jesus Prayer, the answer can only be that to a certain degree (that God alone determines) the possibility exists, at least for those who seek it fervently and with a profound longing.

In its purest form, certainly, it is not accessible to everyone. We know very well that many saints labored and prayed for years without ever being granted the gift of prayer that roots itself in the depths of the heart. Only a very few have ever known the grace and the ineffable joy of pure prayer, in which the *nous* (the spiritual intellect) itself is transcended and the soul dwells with joyous ecstasy in perfect communion with God. "He who has not transcended himself," St Maximus the Confessor holds, "and has not transcended all that is in any way subject to intellection, and has not come to abide in the silence beyond intellection, cannot be entirely free from change," that is, cannot enjoy perfect and unending stillness in blissful union with God.[10] Intellection, the faculty of the *nous* that allows it to apprehend spiritual realities directly, must itself be surpassed. Where this occurs, there a person comes to experience "the sound of sheer silence," the "silence beyond intellection" that enables one's entire being to be flooded with that perfect divine love which is the very being and life of the triune God.

For those of us who will never attain to such heights, there is still abundant hope and an abundant promise. Any one of us, if we desire it enough to pray for it without ceasing, can acquire some measure of the gift of silence that leads to stillness. And with that gift we acquire ears to hear the voice of God that speaks to us in the silence of our heart.

[10]"First Century on Theology," *The Philokalia*, vol. 2 (London: Faber & Faber, 1981), 131.

14
The Gift of Silence

T HE SECOND-CENTURY LATIN THEOLOGIAN Tertullian declared that the blood of the martyrs is the seed of the Church. This remains true to our day, as witnessed most poignantly by the martyrdom of bishops, priests and laypeople during the Communist era, in Russia, Romania and elsewhere, and in the ongoing persecution of Christians at the hands of Muslim extremists in Africa, Asia and the Middle East.

Toward the end of the third century, however, with increasing tolerance shown to Christians and their faith, literal martyrdom began to wane. The witness it represented (martyr means "witness") increasingly took the form of ascetic struggle—spiritual combat against the demons and our most destructive passions—that would constitute the impetus behind the growth of monasticism. Gradually, the monk, the *monochos* or "unified one," became the true martyr, the true witness to the unseen warfare, which is indispensable for pursuing the narrow way that leads to the kingdom of heaven.

Authentic monasticism thus became the new seed of the Church. Over the centuries it has served as the foundation of Orthodox spiritual and liturgical life, and has thereby proven itself an essential element in Christian existence and for the overall witness of the Church in and to the world.

The growing numbers of monastic communities in the United States and Canada have the potential to continue the centuries-old witness to the need within Christian life to acquire certain virtues commonly associated with the hesychast tradition of prayer: "prayer of the heart," grounded in silence and inner stillness, which can, by a gift of pure grace, lead one—monk or layperson—into a deep and abiding communion with the God of love.

If there is one element of traditional monastic experience that is more difficult than any other to acquire in our culture, it is surely the element of silence. Silence lies at the heart of ascetic, and particularly hesychast, tradition and experience. Yet it is all too often misunderstood and neglected, not only by our busy laypeople, but also by monastics, those who have dedicated themselves to a life of witness and prayer.

Therefore, I would like to address, in a very modest and inadequate way, the virtue—the divine gift—of silence. This, unfortunately, is no personal testimony. I make no claim at all to understand the mystery of silence, much less to practice it. The following few sets of reflections are drawn, rather, from the Church's scriptural and ascetic tradition, and from the witness of spiritual elders whose lives have been shaped and blessed by genuine silence. We begin with the experience of silence as it was known in ancient Israel.

There is an obvious and deep irony in any attempt to talk about silence. It's like trying to describe the ineffable or depict the invisible. The task itself is inherently impossible. Silence can only speak for itself: not through words, but through experience. The best way to begin, therefore, is not by any definition or analysis, but by a story.

There is a familiar little account in the alphabetical collection of traditions that have come down to us from the desert fathers of the early Christian centuries. It is said that one day Abba

Theophilus, who was an archbishop, came to Scetis, a desert
wasteland and spiritual paradise, where great numbers of monks
carried on their unseen spiritual warfare. Archbishop Theophilus
made his way to the cell of Abba Pambo, a man recognized and
acclaimed for his humility and wisdom. The brethren who accompanied Theophilus said to Abba Pambo, "Say something to the
archbishop, so that he may be edified." Abba Pambo replied: "If he
is not edified by my silence, he will not be edified by my speech."[11]

There is really little more that can or should be said. If people
are not edified by our silence, then they will not be edified by
our words.

In the beginning there was absolute silence. Through His Word,
God spoke into this silence, to create the heavens and the earth.
Then, on the cosmic Sabbath known as "the seventh day," God
rested. His Word, however, has continued its creative activity
throughout human history. As God declares through the prophet
Isaiah, "My Word that goes forth from my mouth will not return to
me empty; it shall accomplish that which I purpose and succeed
in the thing for which I sent it" (Is 55:11). To affirm that God creates *ex nihilo* is to say that He speaks out of silence, to bring all
things into existence by the power of His creative Word. Word and
silence, then, complement each other. Silence, in the most posi-
tive sense, is the environment and atmosphere, the sacred space,
into which God speaks His Word, both to create the world and to
save it from death and corruption.

Further on in Old Testament tradition, silence becomes the
medium for divine revelation. In a terrifying epiphany recounted
in the first Book of Kings, God appeared on a mountain to the
prophet Elijah. As the Lord passed by, there came a mighty wind,
so strong it split the mountain and shattered the rocks in pieces.
But, the narrative tells us, "the Lord was not in the wind." After the
wind there came an earthquake, then a fire; but the Lord was in

[11]Benedicta Ward, *Sayings of the Desert Fathers: The Alphabetical Collection* (London:
Mowbrays, 1975), 69.

neither. Then, the passage concludes, "after the fire a still, small voice" (1 Kg 19:12). The New Revised Standard Version renders this more forcefully: "after the fire the sound of sheer silence." Through this paradoxical image—"the sound of sheer silence"—God reveals both His presence and His purpose.

From the time of Elijah through the period of classical prophecy, God continued to reveal Himself through His Word of blessing and judgment. At the same time, silence was increasingly perceived as something negative: the absence of God's voice and thus of His presence. "The land of silence" became synonymous with Sheol, the place of the dead where, by definition, the life-giving God is not to be found (Ps 88:11–13; 93:17, LXX). God's judgment pronounced against the nations includes the withering command: "Sit in silence, and go into darkness, daughter Chaldea!" (Is 47:5). Silence is darkness, and that darkness is death.

Finally, Israel itself experiences such a judgment, when the tongues of prophets fall silent as God withdraws His prophetic Word from the people's midst. (The post-Exilic Psalm 73:9 laments, "We do not see our signs; there is no longer any prophet . . ."; cf. 1 Maccabees 14:41, and 2 Baruch 85:3, for whom "the prophets are sleeping.")

Yet even in the Old Testament silence is recognized to have a profoundly spiritual value. "Be angry but do not sin," the psalmist admonishes, "commune with your own hearts on your bed, and be silent" (Ps 4:4). The Septuagint (LXX) or Greek version of the Hebrew Bible expresses the deeper meaning of this verse by slightly modifying the translation: "Be angry, and do not sin; for what you say in your hearts feel compunction on your beds" (4:5). Genuine compunction arises out of the silence and solitude of one's own bed, where, as St Augustine declares, the heart opens to the outpouring of divine love through the Holy Spirit.

The final word on silence, as it was experienced in ancient Israel, is that of the prophet Zephaniah: "Be silent before the Lord God! For the day of the Lord is at hand" (Zeph 1:7). Silence possesses an eschatological quality insofar as it prepares both heart and mind to receive God in His final coming. The day of the Lord is a day of judgment, symbolized by thunder and fury. But it is also a day of vindication, blessing and the bestowal of everlasting peace. These are qualities both given and received in silence.

Israel perceived the silence of the prophets to be a sign of God's judgment upon the people's rebellion and faithlessness. For early Christians, on the other hand, the falling silent of Israel's prophets presaged a new creation and a new revelation. As St Ignatius of Antioch expressed it some eighty years after our Lord's death and resurrection, "There is one God who manifested Himself through Jesus Christ His Son, who is His Word, proceeding from silence . . ." (*Magnesians* 8:2).

God speaks out of silence at the original creation; He does the same with the new creation in Jesus Christ. The Word of God, whose creative power brought all things from nonexistence into being, brings about the new creation of the Church, the universal Body of Christ. From this point on, the Church will be the primary locus of God's creative activity and self-revelation. It is there that the heart can acquire the gift of silence. And it is there that silence resolves into the inner stillness that allows us truly to hear—and thus to obey—the voice of God.

15

On Silence and Solitude

*I*N THE NEW TESTAMENT LITTLE IS SAID of silence as such. The examples that do exist, however, are striking and significant. The people are reduced to awe-filled silence as they witness Christ's ability to silence his adversaries (Lk 20:26). Jesus, in the presence of His disciples, displays the authority to still the waters and silence the thundering of the waves as a great storm threatens to swamp their boat. He rebukes the wind and the sea: "Peace! Be still!" And, St Mark continues, "the wind ceased, and there was a great calm" (Mk 4:39).

Whether on the open sea or in the human heart, peace requires stillness. In the midst of our own storms and turmoil, Jesus speaks these same words, "Peace, be still!" For those who have ears to hear, who can listen to this commandment and receive it as an invitation, the wind of noise, confusion and tumult ceases, and there comes a great calm.

As in the Old Testament, silence in a New Testament perspective possesses an eschatological quality. It describes the response of those in heaven to the promise of Christ's final judgment and vindication of the righteous, together with creation's ultimate and eternal glorification of God: "When the Lamb opened the seventh seal," the Book of Revelation declares, "there was silence in heaven for about half an hour" (Rev 8:1). That brief moment of silence recalls the awe-filled silence to which Israel is called with the coming of the day of the Lord, a day which promises both judgment and salvation: "Be silent, all flesh, before the Lord," exclaims the prophet Zechariah, "for He has roused Himself from His holy dwelling!" (Zech 2:13; cf. Is 41:1; Zeph 1:7).

This admonition is repeated on Holy Saturday, but there its meaning is completely transformed. Then the Church sings, "Let all mortal flesh keep silence, and in fear and trembling stand; for the King of kings and Lord of lords comes forth, to be slain, to give Himself as food to the faithful." In that profound silence the eschatological warnings of judgment are transformed into a glad promise of salvation, as the Lord offers Himself as Eucharist "for the life of the world."

God speaks out of the depths of His own silence, first to create the world, then to renew the world through the incarnation of His Son. Through the voice of the prophets, including the prophet John of the Book of Revelation, God calls us to silence as well. He invites us to go into our "room," our chosen sacred space, and there to shut the door and pray to our Father who is in secret, assured that our Father who is in secret will answer our prayer (Mt 6:6). In that silence we contemplate the mystery of God's creative and saving work, together with the promise of our eternal salvation. It is in that silence that we can listen to God, hear His voice, discern His will and purpose for our life, and, finally, come to know the truth of a precious insight offered by St Isaac of Nineveh: "Silence is the sacrament of the world to come" (*Letter* 3).

A catena of sayings, drawn at random from the desert ascetics of the early Christian centuries, well expresses the value and necessity of authentic silence, silence of the heart:

A brother asked Abba Pambo if it is good to praise one's neighbor, and the old man said to him, "It is better to be silent."[12]

---

[12]Ward, *Sayings of the Desert Fathers*, 69.

A brother asked Abba Poemen, "Is it better to speak or to be silent?" The old man said to him, "The man who speaks for God's sake does well; but he who is silent for God's sake also does well."[13]

It was said of Abba Agatho that for three years he carried a stone in his mouth until he learned to be silent.[14]

St Diodochos of Photiki, a fifth century anti-monophysite bishop well versed in the desert monastic tradition, explained the purpose and fruit of silence in these words. "Spiritual knowledge comes through prayer, deep stillness and complete detachment. . . ." And he adds, "when the soul's incensive power is aroused against the passions, we should know that it is time for silence, since the hour of battle is at hand."[15]

Silence and stillness are essential to attain spiritual knowledge, to engage in spiritual warfare against the passions and against demonic powers, and to allow the voice of God to be heard. Silence and stillness nevertheless require a certain degree of solitude, a temporary withdrawing from the noise and busyness of the world that cause endless distractions and hinder us in our quest for God. "A brother came to Scetis to visit Abba Moses and asked him for a word. The old man said to him, 'Go, sit in your cell, and your cell will teach you everything.' "[16]

Perhaps the greatest challenge to authentic Orthodox Christian life today, at least in the United States, is to transform the heart and mind, our inner being, into a place of silence and solitude. Silence enables us to hear ineffable speech, the words of God that touch, guide and heal, while solitude makes us aware of the discreet yet infinitely powerful presence of the One who is with us

[13] Ibid., 158.

[14] Thomas Merton, *The Wisdom of the Desert* (London: Sheldon Press, 1974), 30.

[15] St Diodochos of Photiki, "On Spiritual Knowledge," in *The Philokalia*, vol. 1 (London: Faber & Faber, 1979), 255. "Incensive power" refers to an aspect of the soul (*to thymikon*) that manifests itself as anger or wrath: negatively, as those terms are generally used, but positively as a force to combat demonic influence, as the power behind our spiritual struggles.

[16] *Moses* 6; Ward, *Sayings of the Desert Fathers*, 118.

"until the end of the age" (Mt 28:20). These two virtues, silence and solitude, enable us to transcend the emptiness of our life. They open the way to a new state of being that to most people seems paradoxical and unattainable: to be alone yet know no loneliness.

In the noise and confusion of the world around us, apprenticeship in the virtues of silence and solitude transforms us at the deepest level of our being. By the grace of God, it creates of the heart of every person who seeks it, a sacred space, an interior monastic cell, a dwelling place for the Spirit of Truth, who teaches, guides, preserves and blesses us as we journey toward the kingdom of heaven.

16

On Silence and Stillness

LTHOUGH THEY ARE OFTEN USED INTERCHANGEABLY, the terms "silence" and "stillness" are not synonymous. Silence implies in part an absence of ambient noise, together with an inner state or attitude that enables us to focus, to center on the presence of God and to hear His "still, small voice."

To silence, the virtue of stillness adds both tranquility and concentration. Stillness implies a state of bodily rest coupled with the creative tension that enables a person to commune with God in the midst of a crowd. It means openness to the divine presence and to prayer: prayer understood as a divine work accomplished by God Himself. As the apostle Paul insists, it is not we who pray, but the Spirit who prays within us (Rom 8:26).

Most of us are familiar with the nineteenth-century account entitled "The Way of a Pilgrim," and "The Pilgrim Continues His Way." Here an anonymous Russian pilgrim, physically handicapped and with only the most rudimentary education, undertakes a voyage of the heart that will lead him step by step toward the heavenly Jerusalem. His journey is marked by numerous encounters with all sorts of people, several of whom initiate him into the practice of the Jesus Prayer. In the Church's ascetic tradition, that prayer is progressively purified, becoming, in rare and privileged cases, "pure prayer" (*kathera proseuchē*) or "prayer of the heart." As many within that tradition have described it, repetition of the name of Jesus begins with the lips, gradually passes to the mind in a spontaneous outpouring, and finally descends with the mind into the heart, the spiritual center of our being. The hesychast tradition therefore invites us to "stand before God with the mind in the heart," to offer Him intercession, thanksgiving, praise and glorification day and night, without ceasing.

The terms used in this context need to be carefully defined. The word "mind" refers not only to our rational capacity, discursive reasoning and analysis, that is, to the activity of the brain as it is usually understood. "Mind" or "intellect" translates the Greek term *nous*, a notion well described by Bishop Kallistos Ware as "the power of apprehending religious truth through direct insight and contemplative vision." The "heart" he goes on to define as "the deep self; it is the seat of wisdom and understanding, the place where our moral decisions are made, the inner shrine in which we experience divine grace and the indwelling of the Holy Trinity." The heart, he adds, "indicates the human person as a 'spiritual subject,' created in God's image and likeness."[17]

Silence fosters stillness; it is indispensable for stillness. Inner stillness, however, goes beyond silence insofar as its aim is to purify the heart and issue in pure prayer. That purification involves the body in its entirety, because body and soul, like mind and heart, are ultimately inseparable. In the words of St Mark the Ascetic, "The intellect cannot be still unless the body is still also; and the wall between them cannot be demolished without stillness and prayer."[18]

Silence is the prerequisite for inner stillness, and only inner stillness enables us truly to listen to God, to hear His voice, and to commune with Him in the depths of our being. Yet silence and stillness are, like prayer itself, gifts that God can and wants to bestow upon us. The greatest truth about us is that God has

---

[17]"The Theology of Worship," in Kallistos Ware, *The Inner Kingdom* (Crestwood, N.Y.: St Vladimir's Seminary Press, 2000), 61–62.

[18]St Mark the Ascetic (early-fifth century, also known as "Mark the Monk" or "Mark the Hermit"), "On Those Who Think They Are Made Righteous By Works," *The Philokalia*, vol. 1 (London: Faber & Faber, 1979), 128.

created us with a profound longing, a burning thirst for communion with Himself. We can easily pervert that longing into an idolatrous quest for something other than God. Yet God remains faithful even in our times of apostasy. Like the father of the Prodigal Son, he always awaits our return. Once we begin that journey homeward, through repentance and an ongoing struggle against our most destructive passions, God reaches out to embrace, to forgive and to heal all that is broken, wounded and wasted. He reaches into the very fabric of our life, to restore within us the sublime image in which we were made.

In the minds of many people, the virtues of silence and solitude, virtues that lead to stillness or hesychia, should remain the concern only of monastics. With the usual demands on our time and the level of noise pollution we all have to deal with at home, in the streets or at our place of work, these virtues seem to be a luxury we can little afford. Even if we really want to reshape our lives to introduce moments of sacred time and sacred space, the effort seems to be too much. We are too rushed in the morning, too tired at night, and too busy in between, even to say a few prayers or read a few lines of Scripture. How can we be expected to cultivate silence, solitude and an enduring stillness under such conditions?

The question, unfortunately, is usually rhetorical. It represents an objection and a refusal. Nevertheless, for those who desire it, cultivating those virtues, at least to a modest extent, is very possible. It requires a certain discipline and, at first, a good deal of patience. But little by little, the experience of inner stillness creates a longing for God that is self-perpetuating. Gradually it becomes a necessity in our life, like eating, sleeping or breathing. We cannot exist without it.

That stillness, however, is a gift of grace. We cannot fabricate it, but we can take small steps to open ourselves to it. And to those small steps the Spirit responds in abundance.

Each of us will have to discover our own most effective means to acquire a measure of quiet and a disposition toward prayer. For many people, it is enough to select a certain space—an icon corner in the bedroom or study, for example—and to set as far as possible a fixed time each day. Alone, away from phones and other distractions, we can light a candle before an icon, then stand, sit or kneel for a few moments until the inner static dies down. Make a conscious effort to relax muscles and limbs, and breathe deeply and slowly. (This is not yoga and these are not techniques; they are means of reestablishing a natural harmony between mind and body that is too easily lost with the frenetic pace of our daily routine.)

In the quiet of that place, bring your mind and heart to focus on God's presence. Then allow the Holy Spirit to direct your prayer in whatever way is most appropriate, most necessary. Make supplication for your own needs; ask forgiveness for those who have offended you; offer intercession for those you love, for the poor, the sick and the suffering; and in all things, give thanks and praise to the One who shares to the fullest extent the world's pain and grief, including your own. Allow prayers of the Church, including the Psalms, to come to mind insofar as you have been able to commit them to memory. Read a few lines of Scripture and meditate on the message they offer to you personally, in that particular moment. Then close with a brief period of emptiness, that is, a stillness free of words, free of thoughts, and conscious only of His Presence.

The Masoretic or Hebrew version of Psalm 46 speaks of the peace and harmony that will accompany the establishment of God's kingdom, His final reign over all the earth. Verse 11 begins with the familiar exhortation, "Be still and know that I am God!"

That stillness, acquired by simple yet faithful discipline, is both the precondition for prayer and the answer to prayer. On the one hand, it charts a way, a movement, a pilgrimage into the depths of the secret heart. But once established in that sacred space, it reveals the presence of God and makes Him known in all His power, majesty and loving kindness.

17

Witnesses to Silence and Stillness

To close this brief series of reflections on silence, solitude and inner stillness, it seems most appropriate to share a few very modest, personal experiences that I have been blessed with over the years. These involve encounters with unpretentious yet holy persons whose example can guide all of us who long to acquire these virtues or qualities for ourselves.

In the early 1970s a community of French Roman Catholic contemplative sisters invited our family to live among them as we made our entry into the Orthodox Church. These sisters were deeply imbued with Orthodox liturgical and ascetic tradition, to the point that many longed to become Orthodox themselves. My fondest memory of the three years we spent in their midst is of the evening Vespers services. A half hour or more before the office began, sisters and their guests began to enter the chapel. They venerated icons, then knelt on the rug and sat back on their heels to pray in the evening stillness. After the service, those who could do so remained. Again they knelt on the rough hemp rug, settled back on their heels, bowed their heads and prayed. The silence in that place was palpable.

I often wondered why it is that silence is so much deeper when it is shared with others. Why is our prayer so much more focused, so much more intense yet totally simple, when we join together in silent worship before the God of infinite love and compassion?

How is it that in that silence our prayer encompasses each of us in a unique way, so that, in unspoken harmony, we intercede for each other, give thanks for each other, and make offering of each other to the God whose presence and love we sense almost physically, God who is ever Emmanuel, God with us?

This kind of experience is a blessed gift, realized through the presence of the Spirit, who unites us before our Lord in thanksgiving, in supplication and in love. These sisters, and the group of brothers who later joined with them, blessed our lives beyond measure. Yet as I look back, I realize we hardly ever spoke to one another. We passed each other in that wilderness area where the community was located; we nodded and smiled; but we kept quiet, unless there was some specific need to speak. In the silence of the pathway, or of the refectory, or of the chapel, we heard the voice of God, as it were, through the silence of the other person. In that silence we exchanged the unspoken assurance that we were praying for each other. And in that silence I came to realize that holiness exists everywhere, that the so-called "ecumenical problem" can be fully resolved there where people who love Christ and offer Him their unceasing adoration, gather in stillness, to worship together and to listen together for the voice of God.

In the village of Taizé in south-central France there is an ecumenical community of monks who receive thousands of pilgrims each year. Most significant for me on our visits there has been the small village church, a Romanesque structure that dates in part to the eleven hundreds. The stone walls are permeated with centuries of prayer. The hard wood benches oblige concentration, and one can spend hours in that place, listening to the silence, hearing the muted voices of the thousands of villagers who, over the ages, have gathered there to pray.

A small Orthodox monastery on the island of Crete was home to a community of monks until they were slaughtered by invading Axis forces during the Second World War. Now a group of sisters lives and prays there. The grounds are filled with fruit trees and the natural beauty provides an ideal setting for shared words and shared silence. The tragic history of this community some-how enhances the sense of God's presence, of His merciful provi-dence that has created in this place of violence and death a haven of stillness and contemplative prayer. *"Agathos ho Theos!"* a sister calls out to me, "God is good!"

In a hospital room a number of years ago, a close friend lay dying. For years he had rebelled against God and against his Ortho-dox faith, expressing that rebellion by indifference to everything connected with the Church. In the last years of his life he had come home. With the simplicity and openness of a child he now turned his face to God and prayed. You could see in his eyes that God replied.

One day, shortly before he died, we spoke about the need for total surrender in the Christian life. Surrender of our being, our values, our hopes and ambitions, all into the loving hands of our merciful Lord. He was quiet for a while. Then he took a scrap of paper and slowly wrote on it the word "surrender." We stayed together a while longer, saying nothing. There, too, was silence, a silence filled with mutual longing for "the one thing needful" (Lk 10:42). In that silence, our friendship, our love for one another, enabled both of us to know stillness, and in that stillness, to know the presence of God and the unfathomable depths of His love.

Repentance, coupled with inner warfare against the passions, is essential if we are to acquire the gifts of silence and stillness, and from there learn to listen to the voice of God. One weapon that proves especially effective in that warfare is the Prayer of Jesus: frequent, quiet repetition of the Name of the Son of God. That Name, which upholds the universe, constitutes the heart and soul of *hēsychia*, the stillness from which flows the prayer of the heart. The Name of Jesus has the power to lift us from spiritual death to a new life of "righteousness and peace and joy in the Holy Spirit," which the apostle Paul identifies with the kingdom of God (Rom 14:17). It is a Name that possesses such power and grace that it can sustain a person even in the face of physical death. Let me close with another incident that illustrates what I mean.

A sister of the Catholic contemplative community I just mentioned was involved in a near-fatal automobile accident. She was transported to the hospital, and for days she hovered between life and death, comatose and maintained on life-support. Her sisters were by her side day and night, gradually losing hope as she failed to regain consciousness. As the medical team was deciding whether to continue life-sustaining treatment, she stirred and made a sound. The sisters gathered close to her and watched as her lips began to move. While she was still in a state of semiconsciousness, they recognized the words she was forming. Out of the depths of her darkness she was speaking words that, as she later recounted it, preserved her and virtually saved her life: "Seigneur Jésus-Christ, Fils de Dieu, aie pitié de moi!," "Lord Jesus Christ, Son of God, have mercy on me!"

Out of a seemingly impenetrable silence and stillness, she found in the "Name above every name" (Phil 2:9) a strength that sustained her in her struggle from near death to complete recovery. Her experience is a spiritual metaphor for the struggle each of us is called to assume: to speak out of inner stillness the sacred Name of Jesus, and to find there the only true healing of soul and body.

As we speak out of that stillness, we also listen. We listen for ineffable words of love and compassion, of healing and life. These are words God addresses to each of us, without exception. And He does so in the silence of the heart. There He makes known the infinite depths of His love for us, His passionate concern to lead us from brokenness to wholeness and from death to life.

This is the experience of the saints, and it can be our experience as well. All that is required is that we make our own the confession of the Psalmist that foreshadows and informs the entire hesychast tradition: "For God alone my soul waits in silence; from Him comes my salvation" (Ps 61/62:1).

18

The Stone Mason

A
BEARDED MAN IN BLUE COVERALLS is building a wall
around the garden outside my window. It's a low
wall, about a meter high, miraculously taking shape
as one rough stone is laid upon another. The man
seems oblivious to his surroundings: a bucolic valley in the Ver-
cors region of south-central France, where the tall green hills ris-
ing around us flow south and east to merge with the towering Alps.

On the high ground behind this renovated eighteenth- century
farmhouse there sits an Orthodox chapel. Its interior is filled with
splendid frescos and finely carved wooden furniture. A sculpted
iconostasis of white marble casts the reflected light of myriad can-
dles into the darker recesses of the nave. The local resident community is made up of a priest and his family, whose common
ministry consists in welcoming individuals and groups for training in the sacred arts of icon painting, mosaics and wood carving.
This afternoon a couple of neighbors are volunteering their time
to work in an atelier downstairs. For several weeks now they have
been fashioning intricate mosaic slabs to replace the worn carpet
that presently covers the chapel floor. While they work in near
total silence, I quietly watch this fellow build his wall.

A pile of stones, gathered from surrounding fields, is scattered in the grass behind him. He picks one up, turns it several
times to find the flattest surface, then with a hammer chips away

a protruding edge. Taking up a trowel, he scoops wet cement from a wheelbarrow, smoothes a layer onto the wall's upper surface, then sets the stone in place. He taps it a few times with the butt end of the trowel, checks the height against a marked stake, then steps back to assess his work. Satisfied, he turns to select another stone. As he does so, his right hand, with fingers clasped to thumb, comes up to his forehead. Simply, discreetly, he makes the sign of the cross. He's a local *paysan*, an Orthodox Christian, and his work belongs to God. Appropriately, significantly, his name is Emmanuel, "God with us."

Every stone he selects is blessed by that same holy gesture. He has no idea he's being observed. Anyway, it wouldn't matter. He's a stone mason, the keeper of a vanishing tradition, and his life's work is above all to build walls. Unlike some fences, his walls are not to "make good neighbors," but to glorify both God and the earth. As he blesses those stones, he blesses all of creation.

We activists, city people or not, spend most of our time, it seems, trying to *produce*, trying to accomplish something we and others will consider worthwhile. A life worth living—even in the Church—is usually seen as a life of great achievements. We admire and even envy those who rise through the ecclesiastical ranks, or publish an impressive number of books, or make their voice heard with authority in the halls of academia or via web lists and chat rooms. We devote hours, days and years to discovering and realizing our "PIL," our purpose in life. Yet most of us never quite find it, never quite feel satisfied with our lot or what we've done with it. So eventually we burn out from frustration, get divorced, or seek a transfer: a geographic cure that heals nothing. And all the time the message drones in our mind: "God, like other people, will judge me on the basis of my accomplishments." Today's most poignant existential question is not whether "to be or not to be?," but rather "to do or not to do?" Yet paradoxically, more is accomplished by being than by doing. At least more that's worthwhile.

Right now Emmanuel is hosing water into a slowly revolving cement mixer. The wall he's building is purely decorative. It serves no real purpose at all, other than to rim the garden with something beautiful. He has spent his life creating walls like this, and he'll most likely go on doing so until his muscles are too weak to lift up the heavy stones and his frame too withered to move the cement-filled barrow. In the minds of most people, he will have lived a rather dull and fruitless life, with little to show for it other than a few basically useless walls.

To those who can see into the depths of his doing and being, however, Emmanuel will continue to bless creation itself with every stone he selects. His efforts, rhythmic and repetitive, will go on producing works of ageless, natural beauty. And some day, in God's good time, he will die—having led a simple, quiet and blessed life that was truly worth living.

19

"With All the Saints"

THE ORTHODOX LITURGICAL CALENDAR is filled with the names of obscure people we know little or nothing about. Some of those names are composites. They are stereotypes based on real persons, usually confessors or martyrs, whose personal history is lost to us, but who come down to us in the Church's collective memory as courageous witnesses to the Faith.

Many others, though, and especially more recent figures, have very specific profiles. We know them much as we know our own ancestors, by virtue of their words and the recollections of their contemporaries that have been transmitted to us as part of our liturgical heritage. When we make the effort to "know" these people—to identify in some personal way with them, with their particular struggles and victories—we discover that they are not merely figures of the past. They are a living presence: persons whom we actually experience and with whom we enter into a shared fellowship in Christ. They acquire a face, even a personality. When our vision of reality expands enough, we become aware that they constantly accompany us and intercede for us. Then they become more than acquaintances. In the best of cases, they become treasured friends.

Every year around August 9, pilgrims gather in Kodiak, Alaska, to celebrate the life and ministry of St Herman, America's first canonized saint. For three years in the mid-70s, my family and I had the privilege of serving in Kodiak at the St Herman's Seminary. On Thursday evenings, with students and parishioners, we stood around the reliquary containing Father Herman's relics and sang the *akathist* hymn. More than the rest of us, the older Native people of the parish "knew" the Elder personally and intimately. They invoked his name each day, entrusted themselves and their family to his intercession, and talked about him to one another as if he were still living in the dense forest of Spruce Island. They still do so today, just as they recall the healing miracles he accomplished and the kind gestures he so often made, offering cookies to village children and consoling people in distress. Death never dimmed this North Star of Christ's Holy Church. It just made all of us look a little farther, a little deeper, to find him very much alive and present in the eternal communion of saints and in the midst of our daily lives.

Thanks to Father Sophrony, we have today a marvelous and deeply moving collection of teachings from the Athonite monk Silouan, as well as Sophrony's brilliant elaborations of those teachings. We know a great deal about Silouan's life: his somewhat troubled youth, his extraordinary vision of the living Christ, and his continual struggle toward sanctity. He inspires us because he is so close to us. And we feel close to him because of our own struggles and doubts, together with the small victories that give us hope that we, too, might attain some measure of inner peace and even holiness.

A great many other saints, recently canonized, are known to us in a profoundly personal way, thanks to biographies compiled on the basis of memories preserved by their contemporaries. We think, for example of Mother Elizabeth and her companions, singing hymns from the bottom of the mine shaft into which they were thrown by Communist authorities, a place that would become their tomb. Or Mother Maria, the "rebel nun," who spent decades in service to the poor and marginalized in France, then literally laid down her life for a friend in a Nazi concentration camp. Or the not-yet-canonized Father Alexander Men, whose brilliant theological and pastoral writings have touched us as much as the tragic, violent death that made of him, too, a modern martyr.

I can't help believing, though, that the communion of saints is made up of multitudes of people whose names will never figure on our liturgical calendars. Each of us has memories of departed persons who have influenced and blessed our lives in immeasurable ways, because of their faith, their wisdom and their love. Persons who are present with us, not just in memory, but also in our immediate, most concrete experience.

I remember especially a beloved Swiss couple who became ersatz grandparents for our children during the years we lived abroad. He was a pastor in the Reformed Church and secretly longed to become Roman Catholic. But God had placed him where he was, and he struggled mightily to remain faithful to that calling. Every morning his wife got up around six, to spend an hour or so reading her worn Bible and praying for everyone in her field of spiritual vision. Decades earlier she had lost a lung and a half to TB and could hardly get around. So she spent most of her time each day on the phone, talking to friends and especially to those in physical or spiritual pain. This couple, each in their own way, graced our lives with their welcoming smiles and boundless affection. They prayed for us then, and I'm sure they do so now, just as they offer ceaseless intercession for all those whom God placed on their path during their time on earth.

My *Doktorvater* (thesis advisor) in Germany was a disciple of Rudolf Bultmann and a scholar through and through. In the lecture hall he was pure historical criticism, but when he visited a quasi-monastic Lutheran community we knew well, he spoke of angels. As a young soldier in the German army during World War II (and associated with the anti-Nazi *Bekennende Kirche*), he found himself pinned down on the Russian front, together with a few acquaintances from his days in the theological faculty in Heidelberg. With other soldiers, they were trapped in a pit, certain that the advancing Russian troops would find them and shoot them on the spot. As what they assumed would be their final gesture, they reached into the bottom of the trench and scooped up a little muddy water. This they combined with a few scraps of moldy bread, in order to celebrate together the Lord's Supper. In their Lutheran tradition they hadn't talked very much about Real Presence. But each one knew that in those simple elements Christ was with them, as nothing less than a living and saving presence. After they were captured and evacuated to Russia, they spent the next four years at hard labor in the gulag. During that time, they took pieces of toilet paper and bits of charcoal, and wrote out as much of the New Testament as they could remember. When these precious manuscripts were found and confiscated, they began again. It preserved their sanity, and it confirmed repeatedly that they were in the very real presence of Christ and the saints. It was there, too, that my mentor discovered that he was visited by angels.

Biographies of saints and of other holy people can mark our lives in very direct and profound ways. They help us to remember—to relive—their witness and to experience their ongoing intercession on our behalf. It is so easy for us to repeat the words of the liturgy in some rote fashion, oblivious to what we are saying. But the living memory of these people, canonized or not, reconfirms for us that we not only commemorate but actually summon in our prayer the Holy Mother of God, and with her the entire communion of saints. As Orthodox Christians, our firmest conviction and surest experience is that "God is with us." But so is she, and so are they.

20

Longing for God

NOSTALGIA IS UNIVERSAL. Rumors abound that it afflicted even the likes of Stalin and Hitler. The term is generally defined as a sentimental yearning for some irretrievable experience or condition, such as bouncing playfully on the knee of our long-deceased grandfather, or singing bawdy ballads in the old fraternity bar, or going home again.

There is another emotion that is often confused with nostalgia but represents something really quite different, more profound and more spiritual. It is the experience of longing. The French have only the word "nostalgie," or possibly *désir*, to cover this entire range of feelings. The Germans, on the other hand, can speak of *Sehnsucht*. This calls up images of a passionate quest, grounded in an insatiable desire, an ardent yearning for something or someone out of reach yet tantalizingly near. As a verb, it's reflexive. "Ich sehne mich nach ihr," a young German boy pines, dreaming longingly of his beloved. In other languages, too, there are special terms, both verbs and nouns, that express this unique and powerful longing for a desired person, the reliving of a precious memory, or the fulfillment of a distant hope.

Longing is more than a psychological condition or an emotional response to some stimulus from our past or future. It is a profoundly spiritual state that finds its closest analogy in the realm of sexual experience. Yet it transcends the purely sexual as much and as fully as hope transcends despair or life transcends death.

In the Church's ascetic tradition, such longing is expressed as *erōs*, an intense desire or aspiration that moves the soul toward communion with the God of love. It commonly involves an element of ecstasy, in which one's very being is transcended to the point that, like the apostle Paul, a person in prayer knows not whether they are "in the body or out of the body" (2 Cor 12), a question to which only God knows the answer.

More frequently, authentic longing is experienced as what Greek tradition calls *charmolupē*, "bright sadness" or "sorrowful joy." In the seventh step of his *Ladder of Divine Ascent*, St John of Sinai (†c. 650) describes this condition as a "mourning that leads to joy." There he says:

> Mourning, according to God, is sadness of soul, and the disposition of a sorrowing heart, which ever madly seeks that for which it thirsts; and when it fails in its quest, it painfully pursues it, and follows in its wake grievously lamenting. Or thus: mourning is a golden spur in a soul which is stripped of all attachment and of all ties, fixed by holy sorrow to watch over the heart . . .

> Keep a firm hold of the blessed joy-grief (*charmolupē*) of holy compunction, and do not stop working at it until it raises you high above the things of this world and presents you pure to Christ.[19]

Most of us, at one time or another, have been given a taste of this kind of longing. We enter one year, for example, as a gift of pure grace, into an especially intense reliving of the events of Holy Week. Immersed in the beauty of the liturgical services, our worship takes on a richness and depth we otherwise rarely know. We become truly conscious of our sinful state: attitudes and actions that drive us away from the mercy and love of our compassionate Father, and that drive us away, too, from others whom we love.

[19]Trans. by Archim. Lazarus Moore (Willits, Calif.: Eastern Orthodox Books, 1973), 113–114).

That love, as we so bitterly know, quickly fades before concerns and preoccupations that lead us to focus almost exclusively upon ourselves. Compunction seizes our heart and conveys a crushing sense of loss: loss of loved ones, loss of purpose, loss of God. And in the midst of a service that is achingly beautiful, we weep. We grieve the losses, the terrible losses, which we have brought upon ourselves, and those that have simply happened for reasons beyond our understanding.

It seems to be God's will, nevertheless, that those tears be accompanied by a quiet inner joy. Mourning truly does lead to joy, insofar as compunction leads to repentance, a turning again from the Old Adam to the New, from the emptiness of self to the *plērōma*, the divine fullness of Christ.

Yet that joy inevitably retains an element of sadness. In this life, holy *erōs* is never pure desire. It is always tempered by the realization that the object of our deepest longing remains beyond our grasp. And for this, curiously but emphatically, we give thanks. For it is precisely the inaccessibility of what we long for that makes the longing so intense, the experience of grief so poignant, and the desire for repentance—for a thoroughgoing return—so genuine. This is what produces the paradoxical mingling of sadness and joy, compunction and ecstasy. The two must be held together and experienced as a single motivating impulse that takes us beyond ourselves, our self-centered values and priorities, and directs our mind and heart toward the Other, whose love we long to know beyond all else.

God calls us not only to life, but also to joy. Longing is the heartrending emotion that tells us that such joy will never be ours until God Himself grants the petition, "Thy kingdom come!" In the meantime, we wait, we pray and we hope. With St Augustine, we remind ourselves: "our hearts are restless until they find their rest in Thee." And we beg God without ceasing to preserve within us the flame of longing: the passionate, ardent yearning to step beyond this world, and to enter at last into all the beauty and all the joy of the world to come.